D0790176
Italian
phrasebook

**Consultant**
Clelia Boscolo

First published 1993
This edition published 2007

Reprint 10 9 8 7 6 5 4 3 2 1
Typeset by Davidson Pre-Press, Glasgow
Printed in Malaysia by Imago

www.collinslanguage.com

ISBN 13 978-0-00-724671-7

## Using your phrasebook

Your *Collins Gem Phrasebook* is designed to help you locate the exact phrase you need, when you need it, whether on holiday or for business. If you want to adapt the phrases, you can easily see where to substitute your own words using the dictionary section, and the clear, full-colour layout gives you direct access to the different topics.

**The Gem Phrasebook includes:**

- Over 70 topics arranged thematically. Each phrase is accompanied by a simple pronunciation guide which eliminates any problems pronouncing foreign words.

- A Top ten tips section to safeguard against any cultural faux pas, giving essential dos and don'ts for situations involving local customs or etiquette.

- Practical hints to make your stay trouble free, showing you where to go and what to do when dealing with everyday matters such as travel or hotels and offering valuable tourist information.

- Face to face sections so that you understand what it is being said to you. These example mini-dialogues give you a good idea of what to expect from a real conversation.

- Common announcements and messages you may hear, ensuring that you never miss the important information you need to know when out and about.

- A clearly laid-out 3000-word dictionary means you will never be stuck for words.

- A basic grammar section which will enable you to build on your phrases.

- A list of public holidays to avoid being caught out by unexpected opening and closing hours, and to make sure you don't miss the celebrations!

It's worth spending time before you embark on your travels just looking through the topics to see what is covered and becoming familiar with what might be said to you.

Whatever the situation, your *Gem Phrasebook* is sure to help!

# Contents

# Pronouncing Italian

Spelling and pronouncing Italian are easy once you know the few basic rules. This book has been designed so that as you read the pronunciation of the phrases, you can follow the Italian. This will help you to recognize how Italian is pronounced and give you a feeling for the rhythm of the language. Here are a few rules you should know:

| Italian | sounds like | example | pronunciation |
|---|---|---|---|
| **au** | ow | ***autobus*** | ow-tobus |
| **ce** | che | ***cena*** | chayna |
| **ci** | chee | ***cibo*** | cheebo |
| **che** * | kay | ***barche*** | barkay |
| **chi** * | kee | ***chiave*** | kee-avay |
| **ge** | jay | ***gelato*** | jay-lato |
| **gi** | jee | ***gita*** | jeeta |
| **ghe** * | gay | ***traghetto*** | tra-get-to |
| **ghi** * | gee | ***ghiaccio*** | geeat-cho |
| **gli** | lyee | ***degli*** | del-yee |
| **gn** | ny | ***ragno*** | ranyo |
| **iu** | yoo | ***aiuto*** | a-yooto |
| **sc(e/i)** | sh | ***scena*** | shayna |
| **sch** * | sk | ***schermo*** | skermo |

* **c** and **g** are hard except when followed by **e** or **i** – to make them hard in Italian an **h** is added.

Double letters **ss**, **tt**, **ll**, etc. are distinctly pronounced – with a slight pause between the two: **posso** pos-so, **gatto** gat-to, **pelle** pel-lay.

Stress usually falls on the next-to-last syllable. We have indicated the stressed syllable with bold in the pronunciation of the phrases.

# Top ten tips

1 Shorts are unacceptable in public in towns and cities, acceptable at the seaside or in holiday resorts. You may not be admitted into a church wearing shorts or even a sleeveless top.

2 Italians talk, by English standards, louder: this does not mean they are always arguing!

3 Italians are genuinely interested and curious about other people, so don't be surprised or put out by intense looks or small talk by strangers.

4 'Ladies first' is a MUST – you must always let them go first.

5 In a public, enclosed space such as a lift, it is polite to acknowledge other people by saying '**Buongiorno**' or '**Buonasera**'.

6 Do not use the familiar '**tu**' form with waiters, however young, shop assistants or hotel staff.

7 In restaurants, wait until everyone has been served before you start eating. When the first course is pasta or pizza, you don't have to wait!

8 When you get introduced to an adult, you have to shake hands; kissing is only for friends.

9 When addressing elders or people you have been just introduced to, use the formal '**Lei**' mode of address.

10 You will rarely see cappuccino ordered at any time other than breakfast.

# Talking to people

## Hello/goodbye, yes/no

Italians can be quite formal in their greeting. If you don't know someone well, the best greeting is **buon giorno** (literally good day). If you are slightly unsure how formal to be **salve** is a good option. **Ciao** is used among family and friends.

| | |
|---|---|
| Please | **Per favore**<br>payr fa-**vo**ray |
| Thanks (very much) | **Grazie (mille)**<br>**grats**-yay (**meel**-lay) |
| You're welcome! | **Prego!**<br>**pray**go! |
| Yes | **Sì**<br>see |
| No | **No**<br>**no** |
| Yes, please | **Sì, grazie**<br>see, **grats**-yay |
| No, thanks | **No, grazie**<br>**no, grats**-yay |

| | |
|---|---|
| OK! | **Va bene!**<br>va **be**nay! |
| Sir/Mr... | **Signore/Signor...**<br>seen-**yo**ray/seen-**yo**r... |
| Madam/Mrs.../ Ms... | **Signora**<br>seen-**yo**ra |
| Miss | **Signorina**<br>seenyo-**ree**na |
| Hello | **Buon giorno/Salve**<br>bwon **jor**no |
| Goodbye | **Arrivederci**<br>ar-reevay-**der**chee |
| Hi/Bye | **Ciao**<br>chow |
| See you later | **A più tardi**<br>a pyoo **tar**dee |
| Good evening | **Buona sera**<br>**bwo**na **say**ra |
| Goodnight | **Buona notte**<br>**bwo**na **not**-tay |
| See you tomorrow | **A domani**<br>a do-**ma**nee |
| Excuse me!/ Sorry! | **Scusi!/Mi scusi!**<br>**skoo**zee!/mee **skoo**zee! |
| Excuse me! (to get past in a crowd) | **Permesso!**<br>per-**mes**-so! |
| How are you? | **Come sta?**<br>**ko**may sta? |

| | |
|---|---|
| Fine, thanks | **Bene, grazie**<br>**be**nay, **grats**-yay |
| And you? | **E Lei?**<br>ay lay? |
| I don't understand | **Non capisco**<br>non ka-**pees**ko |
| I don't speak Italian | **Non parlo italiano**<br>non **par**lo eetal-**ya**no |

# Key phrases

| | |
|---|---|
| the (masculine/ feminine) | **il/la/l'** (+vowel)<br>eel/la/l' |
| the (plural masculine/ feminine) | **i/le**<br>ee/lay |
| the museum | **il museo**<br>eel moo-**zay**o |
| the station | **la stazione**<br>la stats-**yo**nay |
| the shops | **i negozi**<br>ee neg**ots**-ee |
| the houses | **le case**<br>lay **ka**zay |
| a/one (masculine) | **un**<br>oon |
| (feminine) | **una**<br>oona |

| | |
|---|---|
| a ticket/ one stamp | **un biglietto/un francobollo** oon beel-**yet**-to/oon franko**bol**-lo |
| a room/ one bottle | **una camera/una bottiglia** oona kamayra/oona bot-**teel**ya |
| some (masculine/ feminine) | **del/della** del/**del**-la |
| some (plural masculine/ feminine) | **dei/delle** day/**del**-lay |
| some wine | **del vino** del **vee**no |
| some fruit | **della frutta** **del**-la **froot**-ta |
| some biscuits | **dei biscotti** day bees-**kot**-tee |
| some crisps | **delle patatine** **del**-lay pa-ta-**tee**nay |
| Do you have...? | **Avete...?** a-**vay**tay...? |
| Do you have a timetable? | **Avete un orario?** a-**vay**tay oon o**rar**-yo? |
| Do you have a room? | **Avete una camera?** a-**vay**tay oona **ka**-mayra? |
| Do you have milk? | **Avete del latte?** a-**vay**tay del **lat**-tay? |
| I'd like... | **Vorrei...** vor-**ray**... |
| We'd like... | **Vorremmo...** vor-**rem**-mo... |

| | |
|---|---|
| I'd like an ice cream | **Vorrei un gelato**<br>vor-**ray** oon jaylato |
| We'd like to go home | **Vorremmo andare a casa**<br>vor-**rem**-mo andaray a kaza |
| Another/Some more... (singular) | **Dell'altro(a)...**<br>dayl-**lal**tro(a)... |
| (plural) | **Altri(e)...**<br>**al**tree(ay)... |
| Some more bread | **Dell'altro pane**<br>dayl-**lal**tro panay |
| Some more glasses | **Altri bicchieri**<br>**al**tree beek-**yer**ee |
| Another espresso | **Un altro caffè**<br>oon **al**tro kaf-**fe** |
| Another beer | **Un'altra birra**<br>oon **al**tra **beer**-ra |
| Some more water | **Dell'altra acqua**<br>dayl-**lal**tra **ak**wa |
| How much is it? | **Quant'è?**<br>kwan-**te**? |
| How much does it cost? | **Quanto costa?**<br>**kwan**to **kos**ta? |
| large | **grande**<br>**gran**day |
| small | **piccolo**<br>**pee**-kolo |
| with | **con**<br>kon |

| | |
|---|---|
| without | **senza**<br>**sent**sa |
| Where is...? | **Dov'è...?**<br>dov-**e**...? |
| Where are...? | **Dove sono...?**<br>**dov**ay sono...? |
| the nearest | **il/la più vicino(a)**<br>eel/la pyoo vee-**chee**no(-na) |
| How do I get...? | **Per andare...?**<br>payr an-**da**ray...? |
| to the museum | **al museo**<br>al moo-**zay**o |
| to the station | **alla stazione**<br>**al**-la stats-**yo**nay |
| to Milan | **a Milano**<br>a mee**la**no |
| There is... | **C'è...**<br>che... |
| There are... | **Ci sono...**<br>chee sono... |
| There isn't... | **Non c'è...**<br>non che... |
| There aren't any... | **Non ci sono...**<br>non chee sono... |
| When? | **Quando?**<br>**kwan**do? |
| At what time...? | **A che ora...?**<br>a kay **o**ra...? |

| | |
|---|---|
| today | **oggi**<br>**od**jee |
| tomorrow | **domani**<br>do-**ma**nee |
| Can I...? | **Posso...?**<br>**pos**-so...? |
| smoke | **fumare**<br>foo**ma**ray |
| taste it | **provarlo**<br>pro**var**lo |
| How does this work? | **Come funziona?**<br>**ko**may foonts-**yo**na? |
| What does this mean? | **Che cosa vuol dire questo?**<br>kay **ko**za vwol **dee**ray **kwes**to? |



# Signs and notices

| | |
|---|---|
| **ingresso** | entrance |
| **entrata** | entrance |
| **uscita** | exit |
| **aperto** | open |
| **chiuso** | closed |
| **caldo** | hot |
| **freddo** | cold |
| **tirare** | pull |
| **spingere** | push |

| **acqua non potabile** | not drinking water |
|---|---|
| **si prega di...** | please |
| **vietato** | forbidden |
| **libero** | free,vacant |
| **occupato** | engaged |
| **attenti al cane** | beware of the dog |
| **uomini** | gents |
| **donne** | ladies |
| **fuori servizio** | out of order |
| **cassa** | cash desk |
| **noleggio** | for hire/to rent |
| **divieto di balneazione** | no bathing |
| **in vendita** | for sale |
| **saldi** | sale |
| **seminterrato** | basement |
| **pianterreno** | ground floor |
| **ascensore** | lift |
| **suonare** | ring |
| **premere** | press |
| **camere** | rooms available |
| **completo** | no vacancies |
| **uscita d'emergenza** | emergency exit |
| **privato** | private |
| **ai treni** | to the trains |
| **biglietti** | tickets |
| **orario** | timetable |
| **alt** | stop |

| | |
|---|---|
| **convalidare il biglietto qui** | validate your ticket |
| **deposito bagagli** | left luggage |
| **arrivi** | arrivals |
| **partenze** | departures |
| **binario** | platform |
| **non fumatori** | non-smoking |
| **fumatori** | smoking |
| **vietato fumare** | no smoking |

# Polite expressions

There are two forms of address in Italian: formal (**Lei**) and informal (**tu**). You should always stick to the formal until you are invited to use the informal.

| | |
|---|---|
| The lunch was delicious | **Il pranzo era ottimo**<br>eel **pran**tso **er**a **ot**-teemo |
| The dinner was delicious | **La cena era ottima**<br>la **chay**na **er**a **ot**-teema |
| This is a gift for you | **Questo è un regalo per lei**<br>**kwes**to **e** oon ray-**ga**lo payr lay |
| Pleased to meet you | **Piacere**<br>pee-a-**chay**ray |
| This is my husband | **Questo è mio marito**<br>**kwes**to **e mee**yo ma-**ree**to |

| | |
|---|---|
| This is my wife | **Questa è mia moglie** |
| | **kwes**ta e **mee**ya **mol**-yay |
| Enjoy your holiday! | **Buone vacanze!** |
| | **bwo**nya va**kant**say! |

# Celebrations

| | |
|---|---|
| I'd like to wish you... | **Vorrei augurarle** (**augurarti** – informal)... |
| | vor-**ray** owgoo-**rar**-lay (owgoo-**rar**-tee)... |
| Happy Birthday! | **Buon compleanno!** |
| | bwon komplay-**an**-no! |
| Happy Anniversary! | **Felice anniversario!** |
| | fel**ee**chay an-neever-**sar**-yo! |
| Merry Christmas! | **Buon Natale!** |
| | bwon na-**ta**lay! |
| Happy New Year! | **Buon Anno!** |
| | bwon **an**-no! |
| Happy Easter! | **Buona Pasqua!** |
| | **bwo**na **pas**kwa! |
| Have a good trip! | **Buon viaggio!** |
| | bwon vee**ad**-jo! |

# Making friends

In this section we have used the familiar form **tu** for the questions.

**FACE TO FACE**

**A Come ti chiami?**
**ko**may tee kee-**a**mee?
What's your name?

**B Mi chiamo...**
mee kee-**a**mo...
My name is...

**A Di dove sei?**
dee **dov**ay say?
Where are you from?

**B Sono inglese, di Londra**
sono een**glay**say, dee Londra
I'm English, from London

**A Piacere!**
pee-a-**chay**ray!
Pleased to meet you!

| | |
|---|---|
| How old are you? | **Quanti anni hai?**<br>**kwan**tee **an**-nee **a**-ee? |
| I'm ... years old | **Ho ... anni**<br>o ... **an**-nee |
| Where do you live? | **Dove abiti?**<br>**dov**ay **a**beetee? |

| | |
|---|---|
| Where do you live? (plural) | **Dove abitate?** **dov**ay abee**ta**tay? |
| I live in London | **Abito a Londra** **A**beeto a **lon**dra |
| We live in Glasgow | **Abitiamo a Glasgow** Abeet-**ya**mo a **glas**go |
| I'm at school | **Vado a scuola** **va**do a **skwo**la |
| I work | **Lavoro** la-**vo**ro |
| I'm retired | **Sono in pensione** sono een pens-**yo**nay |
| I'm... | **Sono...** sono... |
| married | **sposato(a)** spo-**za**to(a) |
| divorced | **divorziato(a)** deevorts-**ya**to(a) |
| widowed | **vedovo(a)** **vay**-dovo(a) |
| I have... | **Ho...** o... |
| a boyfriend | **un ragazzo** oon ra**gats**-so |
| a girlfriend | **una ragazza** oona ra**gats**-a |
| a partner | **un amico(a)** oon a-**mee**ko(a) |

| | |
|---|---|
| I have ... children | **Ho ... figli**<br>o ... **feel**-yee |
| I have no children | **Non ho figli**<br>non o **feel**-yee |
| I'm here... | **Sono qui...**<br>sono kwee... |
| on holiday | **in vacanza**<br>een va-**kant**sa |
| on business | **per lavoro**<br>payr la-**vo**ro |
| for the weekend | **per il weekend**<br>payr lweek**end** |



# Work

| | |
|---|---|
| What do you do? | **Lei che lavoro fa?**<br>lay kay la-**vo**ro fa? |
| Do you like your job? | **Le piace il suo lavoro?**<br>lay pee-**a**-chay eel **soo**-o la-**vo**ro? |
| I'm... | **Sono...**<br>sono... |
| a doctor | **medico**<br>**med**eeko |
| a manager | **direttore**<br>deeret-**to**ray |

> **Leisure/interests** (p 72)

| | |
|---|---|
| a housewife | **casalinga**<br>kasa-**leen**ga |
| I work from home | **Lavoro da casa**<br>la-**vo**ro da **ka**za |
| I'm self-employed | **Lavoro in proprio**<br>la-**vo**ro een **pro**-pree-o |

# Weather

| | |
|---|---|
| **le previsioni del tempo**<br>lay pre-veez-**yo**nee del **tem**po | weather forecast |
| **tempo variabile**<br>**tem**po varee-**a**beelay | changeable weather |
| **bello** **bel**-lo | fine |
| **brutto** **broot**-to | bad |
| **nuvoloso** noovo-**lo**so | cloudy |

| | |
|---|---|
| It's sunny | **C'è il sole**<br>ch**e** eel **so**lay |
| It's raining | **Piove**<br>pee-**o**vay |
| It's snowing | **Nevica**<br>**nay**-veeka |
| It's windy | **Tira vento**<br>**tee**ra **ven**to |
| What a lovely day! | **Che bella giornata!**<br>kay **bel**-la jor-**na**ta! |

| | |
|---|---|
| What awful weather! | **Che brutto tempo!**<br>kay **broot**-to **tem**po! |
| What will the weather be like tomorrow? | **Come sarà il tempo domani?**<br>**ko**may sa-**ra** eel **tem**po do-**ma**nee? |
| Do you think it's going to rain? | **Pensa che pioverà?**<br>**pen**sa kay pee-ovay-**ra**? |
| It's very hot/cold today | **Fa molto caldo/freddo oggi**<br>fa **mol**to **kal**do/frayd-do **od**jee |
| Do you think there will be a storm? | **Pensa che ci sarà un temporale?**<br>**pen**sa kay chee sa-**ra** oon tempo-**ra**lay? |
| Do you think it will snow? | **Pensa che nevicherà?**<br>**pen**sa kay neveekay-**ra**? |
| Will it be foggy? | **Ci sarà la nebbia?**<br>chee sa-**ra** la **neb**-bya? |
| What is the temperature? | **Quanti gradi ci sono?**<br>**kwan**tee **gra**dee chee sono? |

# Getting around

## Asking the way



| | |
|---|---|
| **davanti a** da-**van**tee a | opposite |
| **accanto a** ak-**kan**to a | next to |
| **vicino a** vee-**chee**no a | near to |
| **il semaforo** eel say-**ma**foro | traffic lights |
| **l'incrocio** leen-**kro**cho | crossroads |
| **all'angolo (della via)** al-**lan**golo (**del**-la **vee**-a) | at the corner (of road) |

**FACE TO FACE**

A **Scusi, per andare alla stazione?**
**skoo**zee, payr an-**da**ray **al**-la stats-**yo**nay?
Excuse me, how do I get to the station?

B **Sempre dritto, dopo la chiesa giri a sinistra/ a destra!**
**sem**pray **dreet**-to, **do**po la kee-**e**za **jee**-ree a see-**nee**stra/a **des**tra!
Keep straight on, after the church turn left/right!

**A** **È lontano?**
**e** lon-**ta**no?
Is it far?

**B** **No, duecento metri/cinque minuti**
No, dooaych**ayn**to **may**tree/**cheen**kway meen**oo**tee
No, 200 metres/five minutes

**A** **Grazie!**
**grats**-yay!
Thank you!

**B** **Prego**
**pray**go
You're welcome

| | |
|---|---|
| We're lost | **Ci siamo smarriti**<br>chee see-**a**mo smar-**ree**tee |
| We're looking for... | **Cerchiamo...**<br>cherkee-**a**mo... |
| Is this the right way to...? | **Questa è la via giusta per...?**<br>**kwes**ta **e** la **vee**-a **joos**ta payr...? |
| Can I/we walk there? | **Si può andare a piedi?**<br>see pw**o** an-**da**ray a pee-**e**-dee? |
| How do I/we get onto the motorway? | **Per andare sull'autostrada?**<br>payr an-**da**ray sool-lowto-**stra**da? |
| to the museum? | **al museo?**<br>al moo**zay**-o? |
| to the shops? | **ai negozi?**<br>**a**-ee neg**ots**-ee? |

Can you show me on the map? **Mi può indicare sulla cartina?**
mee pw**o** eendee-**ka**ray **sool**-la kar-**tee**na?

| YOU MAY HEAR... | |
|---|---|
| **Laggiù**<br>la-**joo** | down there |
| **dietro**<br>dee-**e**tro | behind |
| **poi chieda ancora**<br>**po**-ee kee-**e**da an-**ko**ra | then ask again |

# Bus and coach

In cities you buy tickets from tobacconists, kiosks and bars. You must punch them in the machine on board the bus or tram. Village buses are referred to as **la corriera** or **il pullman** (coach).

**FACE TO FACE**

**A** **Scusi, quale autobus va in centro?**
**skoo**zee, **kwa**lay **ow**-toboos va een **chayn**tro?
Excuse me, which bus goes to the centre?

**B** **Il numero quindici**
eel **noo**mayro **kween**deechee
Number 15

**A** **Dov'è la fermata?**
do**vay** la fayr-**ma**ta?
Where is the bus stop?

**B** **Lì a destra**
lee a **day**stra
There, on the right

**A** **Dove posso comprare i biglietti?**
**dov**ay **pos**-so kom-**pra**ray ee beel-**yet**-tee?
Where can I buy the tickets?

**B** **In edicola**
een ay**dee**cola
At the news-stand

| | |
|---|---|
| Is there a bus/ tram to...? | **Scusi, c'è un autobus/ tram per...?**<br>**skoo**zee, ch**e** oon **ow**-toboos/ tram payr...? |
| Where do I catch the bus/tram to...? | **Dove prendo l'autobus/ il tram per...?**<br>**dov**ay **pren**-do **low**-toboos/ eel tram payr...? |
| We're going to... | **Andiamo a...**<br>an-**dya**mo a... |
| How much is it to go...? | **Quanto costa per andare...?**<br>**kwan**to **kos**ta payr an-**da**ray...? |
| to the centre | **in centro**<br>een **chen**tro |
| to the beach | **alla spiaggia**<br>**al**-la spee-**ad**-ja |

| | |
|---|---|
| How frequent are the buses to...? | **Ogni quanto ci sono gli autobus per...?**<br>**on**-yee **kwan**to chee sono lee **ow**-toboos payr...? |
| When is the first/the last bus to...? | **Quando c'è il primo/l'ultimo autobus per...?**<br>**kwan**do ch**e** eel **pree**mo/ **lool**-teemo **ow**-toboos payr...? |
| Please tell me when to get off | **Per favore può dirmi quando devo scendere**<br>payr fa-**vo**ray pw**o** **deer**mee **kwan**do **dev**o **shen**-deray |
| Please let me off | **Per favore mi fa scendere**<br>payr fa-**vo**ray mee fa **shen**-deray |
| This is my stop | **Questa è la mia fermata**<br>**kwes**ta **e** la **mee**ya fer-**ma**ta |

| YOU MAY HEAR... | |
|---|---|
| **Questa è la sua fermata**<br>**kwes**ta **e** la **soo**-a fer-**ma**ta | This is your stop |
| **Prenda la metro, è più veloce**<br>**pren**da la metro, **e** pyoo vel-**o**chay | Take the metro, it's quicker |



> **Luggage** (p 91)

# Metro

Rome and Milan are the only Italian cities with metro systems. Each journey is a flat rate. You save by buying a book of 10 tickets – **un blocchetto di biglietti** (oon blok-**ket**-to dee beel-**yet**-tee).

| | |
|---|---|
| **l'entrata** len-**tra**ta | entrance |
| **l'uscita** loo-**shee**ta | way out/exit |
| **settimanale/mensile** set-tee-men**a**lay/men**see**lay | weekly/monthly |

| | |
|---|---|
| A book of tickets, please | **Un blochetto di biglietti, per favore**<br>oon blok-**ket**-to dee beel-**yet**-tee, payr fa-**vo**ray |
| A 24-hour ticket | **Un biglietto da ventiquattro ore**<br>oon beel-**yet**-to da ventee-**kwat**-tro **o**ray |
| 48-hour | **da quarantotto ore**<br>da kwarant-**ot**-to **o**ray |
| Where is the nearest metro? | **Dov'è la stazione della metropolitana più vicina?**<br>do-**ve** la stats-**yo**nay **del**-la metro-polee-**ta**na pyoo vee-**chee**na? |

| | |
|---|---|
| How does the ticket machine work? | **Come funziona la biglietteria automatica?** komay foonts-**yo**na la beel-yet-tay**ree**-a owto-**ma**-teeka? |
| I'm going to... | **Vado a...** **va**do a... |
| Do you have a map of the metro? | **Avete una piantina della metro?** a-**vay**tay oona peean-**tee**na **del**-la metro? |
| How do I get to...? | **Per andare a...?** payr an-**da**ray a...? |
| Do I have to change? | **Devo cambiare?** **dev**o kamb-**ya**ray? |
| What is the next stop? | **Qual è la prossima fermata?** kwal **e** la **pros**-seema fer-**ma**ta? |

## Train

You must get your ticket validated at the small machines situated at the ends of platforms before you get on board. They are not always very obvious. If you don't get your ticket stamped you are liable to be fined. You can see on the ticket where to insert it and get it stamped. You also need to stamp it for the return part of the journey. This means you can



> **Luggage** (p 91)

buy tickets in advance of your departure date. If you are taking a fast train, check whether there is a supplement to pay.

| | |
|---|---|
| **locale**<br>lo-**ka**lay | slow stopping train (stops at all stations) |
| **diretto**<br>dee**ret**-to | local train (stops at most stations) |
| **espresso**<br>es**pres**-so | express (stops at main stations) |
| **rapido/inter city**<br>**ra**-peedo/**een**tercity | intercity (stops at main stations: supplement) |
| **super rapido**<br>**soo**per **ra**-peedo | high-speed intercity (reservations compulsory) |
| **binario** bee-**nar**yo | platform |
| **biglietteria**<br>beel-yet-tay-**ree**-a | ticket office |
| **orario** o-**rar**yo | timetable |
| **rtd/ritardo**<br>ree**tar**do | delay |
| **deposito bagagli**<br>de**poz**eeto ba**gal**yee | left luggage |

**FACE TO FACE**

A **A che ora c'è il prossimo treno per...?**
a kay **o**ra ch**e** eel **pros**-seemo **tray**no payr...?
When is the next train to....?

B **Alle 17.10**
allay deechas-**set**-ay ay dee-**e**-chee
At 17.10

A **Vorrei tre biglietti, per favore**
vor-**rayee** tray beel-yet-tee, payr fa**vo**ray
I'd like 3 tickets, please

B **Solo andata o andata e ritorno?**
solo an-**da**ta o an-**da**ta ay ree**tor**-no?
Single or return?

| | |
|---|---|
| Where is the station? | **Scusi, dov'è la stazione?**<br>**skoo**zee, **dov**ay la stats-**yo**nay? |
| 1 ticket | **un biglietto**<br>oon beel-**yet**-to |
| 2 tickets | **due biglietti**<br>dooay beel-**yet**-tee |
| to... | **per...**<br>payr... |
| first/second class | **prima/seconda classe**<br>**pree**ma/se**ko**nda **klas**-say |
| smoking/ non smoking | **per fumatori/non fumatori**<br>payr fooma-**to**ree/non fooma-**to**ree |

| | |
|---|---|
| Is there a supplement to pay? | **C'è un supplemento da pagare?**<br>che oon soop-play-**men**to da pa-**ga**ray? |
| I want to book a seat on the super rapido to Rome | **Vorrei prenotare un posto per il super rapido per Roma**<br>vor-**ray** preno-**ta**ray oon **pos**to payr eel **soo**per **ra**-peedo payr **ro**ma |
| Do I have to change? | **Devo cambiare?**<br>**dev**o kamb-**ya**ray? |
| How long is there for the connection? | **Quanto tempo c'è per la coincidenza?**<br>**kwan**to **tem**po ch**e** payr la koeen-chee-**den**tsa? |
| Which platform does it leave from? | **Da quale binario parte?**<br>da **kwa**lay bee**nar**-yo **par**tay? |
| Is this the train for...? | **Scusi, questo è il treno per...?**<br>**skoo**zee, **kwes**to **e** il **tray**no payr...? |
| Does it stop at...? | **Si ferma a...?**<br>see **fer**ma a...? |
| When does it arrive in...? | **A che ora arriva a...?**<br>a kay **o**ra ar-**ree**va a...? |
| Please tell me when we get to... | **Per favore mi dica quando arriviamo a...**<br>payr fa-**vo**ray mee **dee**ka **kwan**do ar-reev-**ya**mo a... |

Train

| | |
|---|---|
| Is there a restaurant car? | **C'è il vagone ristorante?** che eel va**go**-nay reesto-**ran**tay? |
| Is this seat free? | **È libero questo posto?** **e lee**-bero **kwes**to **pos**to? |
| Excuse me! (to get past) | **Permesso!** per-**mes**-so! |

## Taxi

The easiest place to find a taxi stand is at a railway station. Official taxis are generally white.

| | |
|---|---|
| I want a taxi | **Vorrei un taxi** vor-**ray** oon **tak**see |
| Where can I get a taxi? | **Dove posso trovare un taxi?** **dov**ay **pos**-so tro-**va**ray oon **tak**see? |
| Please order me a taxi... | **Per favore mi chiami un taxi...** payr fa-**vo**ray mee kee-amee oon taksee... |
| now | **subito** **soo**-beeto |
| for...(time) | **per le...** payr lay... |



> **Luggage** (p 91)

| | |
|---|---|
| How much will it cost to go to...? | **Quanto verrà a costare per andare a/al/alla** (etc.)**...?**<br>**kwan**to ver-**ra** a kos-**ta**ray payr an-**da**ray a/al/**al**-la...? |
| to the station | **alla stazione**<br>**al**-la stats-**yo**nay |
| to the airport | **all'aeroporto**<br>al-la-ayro-**por**to |
| to this address | **a questo indirizzo**<br>a **kwes**to een-dee**reets**-so |
| How much is it? | **Quant'è?**<br>kwan-**te**? |
| It's more than on the meter | **È più di quanto indicato sul tachimetro**<br>**e** pee-**oo** dee **kwan**to eendee-**ka**to sool ta-**kee**metro |
| Keep the change | **Tenga il resto**<br>**ten**ga eel **res**to |
| Sorry, I don't have any change | **Mi dispiace, non ho moneta**<br>mee deespee-**a**-chay, non o mo-**net**a |
| I'm in a hurry | **Ho fretta**<br>o **fret**-ta |
| I have to catch... | **Devo prendere...**<br>**dev**o **pren**-deray... |
| a train | **il treno**<br>eel **tray**no |
| a plane | **l'aereo**<br>la-**ayr**ay-o |

> **Luggage** (p 91)

# Boat and ferry

You can buy travel cards for Venice (**Carta Venezia**) which allow you to use all the water buses (**vaporetti**).

| | |
|---|---|
| A Venice card for one day | **Una carta Venezia per un giorno**<br>oona **kar**ta ve**nets**eeya payr oon **jor**no |
| two days | **per due giorni**<br>payr **doo**ay **jor**nee |
| How much is it for an hour on the gondola? | **Quanto costa viaggiare in gondola per un'ora?**<br>**kwan**to **kos**ta veead-**jar**ay een **gon**dola payr oon **o**ra? |
| Have you a timetable? | **Ha l'orario?**<br>al o**rar**-yo |
| Is there a car ferry to...? | **C'è il traghetto macchine per...?**<br>ch**e** eel tra-**get**-to **mak**-keenay payr...? |
| How much is a ticket...? | **Quanto costa un biglietto...?**<br>**kwan**to **kos**ta oon beel-**yet**-to...? |
| single | **andata**<br>an-**da**ta |
| return | **andata e ritorno**<br>an-**da**ta ay ree-**tor**no |

| | |
|---|---|
| How much is it for a car and ... people? | **Quanto costa per un'automobile e ... persone?**<br>**kwan**to **kos**ta payr oon owto-**mo**beelay ay ... per-**so**nay? |
| Where does the vaporetto leave from? | **Da dove parte il vaporetto?**<br>da **dov**ay **par**tay eel vapo**ret**-to? |
| for the Lido | **per il Lido**<br>payr eel **lee**do |
| When is the first/ the last boat? | **Quando parte il primo/ l'ultimo battello?**<br>**kwan**do **par**tay eel **pree**mo/ **lool**-teemo bat-**tel**-lo? |

| YOU MAY HEAR... | |
|---|---|
| **Questo è l'ultimo battello**<br>**kwes**to **e** **lool**-teemo bat-**tel**-lo | This is the last boat |
| **Oggi non c'è servizio...**<br>**od**jee non ch**e** ser**veets**-yo... | Today there is no service... |
| **perché c'è lo sciopero**<br>per**kay** ch**e** lo **sho**-pero | because there is a strike |

Boat and ferry

# Air travel

| | |
|---|---|
| **arrivi** ar-**ree**vee | arrivals |
| **partenze** par-**tent**say | departures |
| **internazionali** eenternats-yo**nal**ee | international |
| **nazionali** nats-yo**nal**ee | domestic |
| **imbarco** eem-**bar**ko | boarding gate |

How do I get to the airport? **Scusi, per andare all'aeroporto?**
**skoo**zee payr an-**dar**ay al-la-ayro-**por**to?

Is there a bus to the airport? **C'è l'autobus per l'aeroporto?**
che **low**to-boos payr la-ayro-**por**to?

Where is the luggage for the flight from...? **Scusi, dov'è il bagaglio del volo da...?**
**skoo**zee, do-**ve** eel ba**gal**-yo del **vo**lo da...?

Where can I change some money? **Scusi, dove posso cambiare i soldi?**
**skoo**zee, **dov**ay **pos**-so kamb-**ya**ray ee **sol**dee?

How do I/we get into town? **Scusi, come si va in città?**
**skoo**zee, **ko**may see va een cheet-**ta**?

How much is it by taxi...? **Quanto costa il taxi...?**
**kwan**to **kos**ta eel **tak**see...?

| | |
|---|---|
| to go into town? | **per andare in città?** payr an-**da**ray een cheet-**ta**? |
| to go to the Hotel...? | **per andare all'Hotel...?** payr an-**da**ray al-lo**tel**...? |

| YOU MAY HEAR... | |
|---|---|
| **L'imbarco sarà all'uscita numero...** leem**bar**-ko sa-**ra** al-loo**shee**ta **noo**-mayro... | Boarding will take place at gate number... |
| **Vada subito all'uscita numero...** vada **soo**-beeto al-loo**shee**ta **noo**-mayro... | Go immediately to gate number... |



# Customs control

EU citizens are subject only to spot checks and they can go through the blue customs channel (unless they have goods to declare). There is no restriction, either by quantity or value, on goods purchased by EU travellers in another EU country provided that they are for their own personal use. If you are unsure about certain items, check with the customs officials whether duty is payable.

> **Luggage** (p 91)

| | |
|---|---|
| **cittadini UE**<br>cheeta-**dee**nee oo-ay | EU citizens |
| **altri passaporti**<br>altree pas-sa**por**tee | other passports |
| **la carta d'identità**<br>la karta deedentee-**ta** | identity card |
| **la dogana** la do**ga**na | customs |

| | |
|---|---|
| Do I have to pay duty on this? | **Devo pagare la dogana per questo?**<br>**dev**o pa-**ga**ray la do-**ga**na payr **kwes**to? |
| It's for my own personal use/ a present | **È per uso personale/un regalo**<br>**e** payr **oo**zo perso-**na**lay/ oon ray-**ga**lo |
| We are on our way to... (if in transit through a country) | **Siamo in transito per...**<br>see-**a**mo een **tran**-zeeto payr... |

# Driving

## Car hire

| | |
|---|---|
| **la patente** la pa**ten**-tay | driving licence |
| **la polizza a casco** la po**leet**-sa a kasko | fully comprehensive insurance |

| | |
|---|---|
| I want to hire a car | **Vorrei noleggiare una macchina** vor-**ray** noled-**ja**ray oona **mak**-keena |
| for ... days | **per ... giorni** payr ... **jor**nee |
| with automatic gears | **col cambio automatico** kol **kam**byo owto-**ma**-teeko |
| What are your rates...? | **Quanto costa...?** **kwan**to **kos**ta...? |
| per day | **al giorno** al **jor**no |
| per week | **per settimana** payr set-tee-**ma**na |

| | |
|---|---|
| How much is the deposit? | **Quant'è l'anticipo?**<br>kwan-**te** lan**tee**-cheepo? |
| Do you take credit cards? | **Accettate le carte di credito?**<br>at-chet-**ta**tay lay **kar**tay dee **kray**-deeto? |
| Is there a mileage (kilometre) charge? | **Si paga al chilometro?**<br>see pa-**ga** al kee**lo**-metro? |
| How much is it? | **Quant'è?**<br>kwan-**te**? |
| Does the price include fully comprehensive insurance? | **Il prezzo è inclusivo della polizza a casco?**<br>eel **prets**-so **e** eenkloo-**zee**vo **del**-la po-**leet**sa a **kas**ko? |
| Must I return the car here? | **Devo riportare la macchina qui?**<br>**dev**o reepor-**ta**ray la **mak**-keena kwee? |
| By what time? | **Per quando?**<br>payr **kwan**do? |
| I'd like to leave it in... | **Vorrei lasciarla a...**<br>vor-**ray** la-**sha**rla a... |

**YOU MAY HEAR...**

| | |
|---|---|
| **Riporti la macchina con il serbatoio pieno**<br>ree-**por**tee la **mak**-keena kon eel serba-**to**yo pee**yen**o | Please return the car with a full tank |

# Driving

The speed limits in Italy are 50 km/h in built up areas, 90–110 km/h on main roads, 130 km/h on 2-lane motorways and 140 km/h on 3-lane motorways (except in bad weather and at night). Headlights must be used at all times.

| | |
|---|---|
| Can I/we park here? | **Si può parcheggiare qui?**<br>see pw**o** parked-**ja**ray kwee? |
| How long for? | **Per quanto tempo?**<br>payr kwanto tempo? |
| Which junction is it for...? | **Quale uscita è per...?**<br>**kwa**lay oo-**shee**ta **e** payr...? |
| Do I/we need snow chains? | **Si devono usare le catene da neve?**<br>see **dev**ono oo-**za**ray lay ka-**tay**nay da **nay**vay? |

# Petrol

Many petrol stations are now self-service and you can pay by inserting a banknote/credit card into the appropriate slot on the pump.

| | |
|---|---|
| **gasolio** ga-**zol**yo | diesel |
| **senza piombo** **sen**tsa pee-**om**bo | unleaded |

| | |
|---|---|
| Fill it up, please | **Il pieno per favore** eel pee-**ye**no payr fa-**vo**ray |
| Please check the oil/the water | **Per favore controlli l'olio/ l'acqua** payr fa-**vo**ray kon**trol**-lee **lol**-yo/ **lak**wa |
| 30 euros worth of unleaded petrol | **Trenta euro di benzina senza piombo** **tren**ta ay-**oo**-ro dee bend-**zee**na **sen**tsa pee-**om**bo |
| Where is...? | **Dov'è...?** do-**ve**...? |
| the air line | **la canna dell'aria** la **kan**-na del-**lar**-ee-a |
| water | **la canna dell'acqua** la **kan**-na del-**lak**wa |
| Pump number... | **Pompa numero...** **pom**pa **noo**mayro... |

| | |
|---|---|
| Where do I pay? | **Dove pago?**<br>**do**vay **pa**go? |
| Can I pay by credit card? | **Posso pagare con la carta di credito?**<br>**pos**-so pa-**ga**ray kon la **kar**ta dee **kray**-deeto? |

| YOU MAY HEAR... | |
|---|---|
| **Manca un po' d'olio/ un po' d'acqua**<br>**man**ka oon po **dol**-yo/ oon po **dak**wa | You need some oil/ some water |
| **Tutto a posto**<br>**toot**-to a **pos**to | Everything is OK |

Breakdown

# Breakdown

If you break down, the emergency phone number for the Italian equivalent of the AA (ACI – **Automobile Club d'Italia**) is 116. A garage that does repairs is known as an **autofficina** (owto-of-fee**chee**na).

| | |
|---|---|
| Can you help me? | **Può aiutarmi?**<br>pw**o** a-yoo-**tar**mee? |
| My car has broken down | **La mia macchina è in panne**<br>la **mee**ya **mak**-keena **e** een **pan**-nay |

| | |
|---|---|
| I've run out of petrol | **Non ho più benzina**<br>non o pyoo bend-**zee**na |
| Can you tow me to the nearest garage? | **Può trainarmi fino al prossimo garage?**<br>pw**o** tra-ee-**nar**mee **fee**no al **pros**-seemo ga-**razh**? |
| Do you have parts for a (make of car)...? | **Ha ricambi per la...?**<br>a ree-**kam**bee payr la...? |
| There's something wrong with the... | **C'è qualcosa che non va con il/la/i/le** (etc.)**...**<br>ch**e** kwal-**ko**za kay non va kon eel/la/ee/lay... |
| Can you replace...? | **Può cambiare ...?**<br>pw**o** kamb-**ya**ray ...? |



# Car parts

| | |
|---|---|
| The ... doesn't work | **Il/La ... non funziona**<br>eel/la ... non foonts-**yo**na |
| The ... don't work | **I/Le... non funzionano**<br>ee/lay ... non foonts-**yo**nano |

| | | |
|---|---|---|
| accelerator | **l'acceleratore** | at-chelera-**to**ray |
| alternator | **l'alternatore** | alterna-**to**ray |
| battery | **la batteria** | bat-tay-**ree**-a |
| bonnet | **il cofano** | **ko**-fano |

| | | |
|---|---|---|
| brakes | **i freni** | **fray**nee |
| choke | **l'aria** | **ar**-ya |
| clutch | **la frizione** | freets-**yo**nay |
| distributor | **il distributore** | deestree-boo-**to**ray |
| engine | **il motore** | mo-**to**ray |
| exhaust | **il tubo di scappamento** | **too**bo dee skap-pa-**men**to |
| fuse | **il fusibile** | foo**zee**-beelay |
| gears | **le marce** | **mar**chay |
| handbrake | **il freno a mano** | **fray**no a **ma**no |
| headlights | **i fari** | **fa**ree |
| ignition | **l'accensione** | at-chens-**yo**nay |
| indicator | **la freccia** | **frech**-cha |
| points | **le puntine** | poon-**tee**nay |
| radiator | **il radiatore** | radya-**to**ray |
| reverse gear | **la retromarcia** | retro-**mar**cha |
| seat belt | **la cintura di sicurezza** | cheen-**too**ra dee seekoo-**rets**-sa |
| spark plug | **la candela** | kan-**day**la |
| steering | **lo sterzo** | **ster**tso |
| steering wheel | **il volante** | vo-**lan**tay |
| tyre | **la gomma** | **gom**-ma |
| wheel | **la ruota** | **rwo**ta |
| windscreen | **il parabrezza** | para-**bredz**-za |
| windscreen washer | **il lavacristallo** | lava-kree-**stal**-lo |
| windscreen wiper | **il tergicristallo** | terjee-kree-**stal**-lo |

Car parts

# Road signs

danger

give way

libero
spaces

full

SENSO UNICO
one way

north
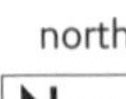

west

east
south

you have right of way

end of right of way

police check

customs

**RALLENTARE**

slow down

switch on headlights

**ZONA PEDONALE**

pedestrian zone

AUTOSTRADA

motorway signs are green in Italy

# Staying somewhere



## Hotel (booking)

Bed and breakfast, particularly on farms and in the countryside, is becoming very popular. You can find out more about **agriturismo** on www.agriturismo.com.

**FACE TO FACE**

**A** **Vorrei prenotare una camera singola/doppia**
vor-**ray** preno-**ta**ray oona **ka**-mayra **seen**-gola/ **dop**-pya
I'd like to book a single/double room

**B** **Per quante notti?**
payr **kwan**tay **not**-tee?
For how many nights?

**A** **per una notte/... notti/dal... al...**
payr oona **not**-tay/... **not**-tee/dal... al...
for one night/... nights/from... till...
**Quant'è per notte/per settimana?**
kwan-**te** payr **not**-tay/payr set-tee-**ma**na?
How much is it per night/per week?

| | |
|---|---|
| Do you have a room for tonight? | **Avete una camera per questa notte?**<br>a-**vay**tay oona **ka**-mayra payr **kwes**ta **not**-tay? |
| with bath | **con bagno**<br>kon **ban**-yo |
| with shower | **con doccia**<br>kon **dot**-cha |
| with a double bed | **con letto matrimoniale**<br>kon **let**-to matree-mon-**ya**lay |
| twin-bedded | **a due letti**<br>a dooay **let**-tee |
| with an extra bed for a child | **con un letto extra per un bambino**<br>kon oon **let**-to **ex**tra payr oon bam-**bee**no |
| Is breakfast included? | **La prima colazione è inclusa?**<br>la **pree**ma kolats-**yo**nay e een-**kloo**sa? |
| I'd like to see the room | **Vorrei vedere la camera**<br>vor-**ray** ve**der**ay la **ka**-mayra |

| YOU MAY HEAR... | |
|---|---|
| **Siamo al completo**<br>see-**a**mo al kom**play**-to | We're full |
| **Il suo nome per favore**<br>eel **soo**-o **no**may payr fa-**vo**ray | Your name, please |

| YOU MAY HEAR... | |
|---|---|
| **La prego di confermare...** la **pray**go dee konfer-**ma**ray... | Please confirm... |
| **per e-mail** payr e-mail | by e-mail |
| **con un fax** kon oon fax | by fax |

# Hotel desk

Many hotels are now signposted in towns. The Italian word for a hotel is **albergo** (al-**ber**go)

| | |
|---|---|
| I booked a room... | **Ho prenotato una camera...** o prayno-**ta**to oona **ka**-mayra... |
| in the name of... | **a nome di...** a **no**may dee... |
| Where can I park the car? | **Dove posso parcheggiare la macchina?** **dov**ay **pos**-so parked-**ja**ray la **mak**-keena? |
| What time is...? | **A che ora è...?** a kay **o**ra **e**...? |
| dinner | **la cena** la **chay**na |

breakfast **la prima colazione**
la **pree**ma kolats-**yo**nay

The key, please **La chiave per favore**
la kee-**a**vay payr fa-**vo**ray

Room number... **Camera numero...**
**ka**-mayra **noo**-mayro...

I'm leaving tomorrow **Parto domani**
**par**to do-**ma**nee

Please prepare the bill **Mi prepari il conto**
mee pre**pa**ree eel **kon**to

# Camping

| | |
|---|---|
| **la spazzatura**<br>la spats-sa**too**ra | rubbish |
| **acqua potabile**<br>**ak**wa po-**ta**beelay | drinking water |
| **la presa di corrente**<br>la **pre**sa dee kor-**ren**tay | electric point |

Is there a restaurant/a self-service café on the campsite? **C'è un ristorante/ un selfservice nel campeggio?**
ch**e** oon reesto-**ran**tay/oon selfservice nel kam**ped**-jo ?

Do you have any vacancies? **Avete dei posti?**
a-**vay**tay day **pos**tee?

| | |
|---|---|
| How much is it per night? | **Quanto costa per notte?** <br> **kwan**to **kos**ta payr **not**-tay? |
| per tent | **per tenda** <br> payr **ten**da |
| per caravan | **per roulotte** <br> payr roo**lot** |
| per person | **per persona** <br> payr per-**so**na |
| Does the price include...? | **Il prezzo include...?** <br> eel **prets**-so eenk**loo**day...? |
| showers/hot water/electricity | **doccia/acqua calda/ elettricità** <br> **dot**-cha/**ak**wa **kal**da/ elet-treechee-**ta** |
| We'd like to stay for ... nights | **Vorremmo rimanere per ... notti** <br> vor-**rem**-mo reema-**ne**ray payr ... **not**-tee |

# Self-catering

| | |
|---|---|
| Who do we contact if there are problems? | **Chi contattiamo se ci sono dei problemi?**<br>kee kontat-**tya**mo say chee sono day pro-**blay**mee? |
| How does the heating work? | **Come funziona il riscaldamento?**<br>**kom**ay foonts-**yo**na eel reeskalda-**men**to? |
| Is there always hot water? | **C'è sempre l'acqua calda?**<br>che **sem**pray **lak**wa **kal**da? |
| Where is the nearest supermarket? | **Dov'è il supermercato più vicino?**<br>do-**ve** eel soopermer**ka**to pyoo vee-**chee**no? |
| Where do we leave the rubbish? | **Dove mettiamo la spazzatura?**<br>**dov**ay met-**tya**mo la spats-sa**too**ra? |



> **Sightseeing and tourist office** (p 70)

# Shopping

## Shopping phrases

Opening hours are approx. 8.30 am to 12.30 pm and 4 to 7.30 pm Mon. to Sat. Opening hours tend to be longer in summer. Some supermarkets are open all day.



**FACE TO FACE**

**A** **Mi dica/Desidera?**
mee **dee**ka/dez-**ee**dayra?
What would you like?

**B** **Avete...?**
a-**vay**tay...?
Do you have...?

**A** **Sì, certo. Ecco a lei. Altro?**
see, **chay**rto. **Ayk**-ko a layee. Altro?
Certainly, here you are. Anything else?

| | |
|---|---|
| Where is...? | **Scusi, dov'è...?** |
| | **skoo**zee do-**ve**...? |
| I'm just looking | **Sto solo guardando** |
| | sto **so**lo gwar-**dan**do |
| I'm looking for a present for... | **Cerco un regalo per...** |
| | **cher**ko oon ray-**ga**lo payr... |
| my mother | **mia madre** |
| | **mee**ya **ma**dray |
| a child | **un bambino** |
| | oon bam-**bee**no |
| Where can I buy...? | **Dove posso comprare...?** |
| | **do**vay **pos**-so kom-**pra**ray...? |
| shoes | **delle scarpe** |
| | **del**-lay **skar**pay |
| gifts | **dei regali** |
| | day ray-**ga**lee |
| Do you have anything...? | **Avete qualcosa...?** |
| | a-**vay**tay kwal-**ko**za...? |
| larger | **più grande** |
| | pyoo **gran**day |
| smaller | **più piccolo** |
| | pyoo **peek**-kolo |
| It's too expensive for me | **È troppo caro per me** |
| | **e trop**-po **ka**ro payr me |
| Can you give me a discount? | **Mi può fare uno sconto?** |
| | mee pw**o far**ay oono **skon**to? |

# Shops

| | |
|---|---|
| **saldi** **sal**dee | sale |
| **sconto** **skon**to | discount |
| **chiuso per ferie** **kyoo**zo payr **fer**-yay | closed for holidays |

| | | |
|---|---|---|
| baker's | **panificio** | panee-**fee**cho |
| butcher's | **macelleria** | machel-lay-**ree**-a |
| cake shop | **pasticceria** | pasteechay-**ree**-a |
| clothes | **abbigliamento** | ab-beelya-**men**to |
| fruit shop | **fruttivendolo** | frut-tee-**ven**-dolo |
| gifts | **regali** | ray-**ga**lee |
| grocer's | **alimentari** | alee-men-**ta**ree |
| hairdresser's | **parrucchiere** | par-rook-**ye**ray |
| newsagent | **giornalaio** | jorn-**la**-ayo |
| optician | **ottico** | **ot**-teeko |
| perfume shop | **profumeria** | pro-foo-may**ree**-a |
| pharmacy | **farmacia** | farma-**chee**-a |
| photographic shop | **fotografo** | fo**to**-grafo |
| shoe shop | **calzature** | kaltsa-**too**ray |
| sports shop | **articoli sportivi** | ar-**tee**-kolee spor-teevee |
| supermarket | **supermercato** | sooper-mer-**ka**to |
| tobacconist's | **tabaccaio** | tabak-**ka**-yo |
| toys | **giocattoli** | jo**kat**-tolee |

Shopping

# Food (general)

| | | |
|---|---|---|
| biscuits | **i biscotti** | bee-**skot**-tee |
| bread | **il pane** | **pa**nay |
| bread roll | **il panino** | pa-**nee**no |
| bread (brown) | **il pane integrale** | panay eenteg-**ra**lay |
| butter | **il burro** | **boor**-ro |
| cheese | **il formaggio** | for**mad**-jo |
| chicken | **il pollo** | **pol**-lo |
| coffee (instant) | **il caffè solubile** | kaf-**fe** so**loo**-beelay |
| cream | **la panna** | **pan**-na |
| crisps | **le patatine** | pata-**tee**nay |
| eggs | **le uova** | **wov**a |
| fish | **il pesce** | **pesh**ay |
| ham (cooked) | **il prosciutto cotto** | pro-**shoot**-to **kot**-to |
| ham (cured) | **il prosciutto crudo** | pro-**shoot**-to **kroo**-do |
| herbal tea | **l'infuso di erbe** | een-**foo**so dee **ayr**bay |
| jam | **la marmellata** | marmel-**la**ta |
| juice, orange | **il succo d'arance** | **sook**-ko da-**ran**chay |
| margarine | **la margarina** | marga-**ree**na |
| marmalade | **la marmellata d'arance** | marmel-**la**ta da-**ran**chay |

| | | |
|---|---|---|
| milk | **il latte** | **lat**-tay |
| olive oil | **l'olio d'oliva** | **ol**-yo do-**lee**va |
| pepper | **il pepe** | **pep**ay |
| salt | **il sale** | **sa**lay |
| sugar | **lo zucchero** | **tsook**-kero |
| tea | **il tè** | t**e** |
| tomatoes (tin) | **la scatola di pelati** | **ska**-tola dee pel-**a**tee |
| vinegar | **l'aceto** | a-**chay**to |
| yoghurt | **lo yogurt** | **yo**gurt |

# Food (fruit and veg)

## Fruit

| | | |
|---|---|---|
| apples | **le mele** | **may**lay |
| apricots | **le albicocche** | albee-**kok**-kay |
| bananas | **le banane** | ba-**na**nay |
| cherries | **le ciliegie** | cheel-**ye**-jay |
| grapefruit | **il pompelmo** | pom-**pel**mo |
| grapes | **l'uva** | **oo**va |
| lemon | **il limone** | lee-**mo**nay |
| melon | **il melone** | mel-**o**nay |
| oranges | **le arance** | a-**ran**chay |
| peaches | **le pesche** | **pes**kay |
| pears | **le pere** | **pe**ray |

Shopping


> **Measurements and quantities** (p 109)

| | | |
|---|---|---|
| plums | **le prugne** | **proon**-yay |
| raspberries | **i lamponi** | lam-**po**nee |
| strawberries | **le fragole** | **fra**-golay |
| watermelon | **l'anguria** | ang-**oo**-ree-a |

## Vegetables

| | | |
|---|---|---|
| asparagus | **gli asparagi** | as**pa**-rajee |
| aubergine | **la melanzana** | melant-**sa**na |
| carrots | **le carote** | ka-**ro**tay |
| cauliflower | **il cavolfiore** | kavolf-**yo**ray |
| celery | **il sedano** | **se**-dano |
| courgettes | **gli zucchini** | tsook-**kee**nee |
| cucumber | **il cetriolo** | chetree-**o**lo |
| garlic | **l'aglio** | **al**-yo |
| leeks | **i porri** | **por**-ree |
| mushrooms | **i funghi** | **foon**gee |
| onions | **le cipolle** | chee**pol**-lay |
| peas | **i piselli** | pee**zel**-lee |
| pepper | **il peperone** | peper-**o**nay |
| potatoes | **le patate** | pa-**ta**tay |
| runner beans | **i fagiolini** | fajo-**lee**nee |
| salad | **l'insalata** | eensa-**la**ta |
| spinach | **gli spinaci** | spee-**na**chee |
| tomatoes | **i pomodori** | pomo-**do**ree |

# Clothes

| women's sizes | | men's suit sizes | | shoe sizes | | | |
|---|---|---|---|---|---|---|---|
| UK | EU | UK | EU | UK | EU | UK | EU |
| 8 | 36 | 36 | 46 | 2 | 35 | 7 | 41 |
| 10 | 38 | 38 | 48 | 3 | 36 | 8 | 42 |
| 12 | 40 | 40 | 50 | 4 | 37 | 9 | 43 |
| 14 | 42 | 42 | 52 | 5 | 38 | 10 | 44 |
| 16 | 44 | 44 | 54 | 6 | 39 | 11 | 45 |
| 18 | 46 | 46 | 56 | | | | |



**FACE TO FACE**

A **Posso provarlo?**
**pos**-so pro-**var**lo?
May I try this on?

B **Prego, si accomodi**
**pray**go, see ak-**ko**modee
Please come this way

A **Ha una taglia ...**
a oona **tal**-ya ...
Do you have a ...
**piccola/media/grande?**
**peek**-kola/**med**-ya/**gran**day?
small/medium/large size?

**Che taglia porta?**
kay **tal**-ya **por**ta?
What size (clothes) do you take?
**In questo colore c'è solo questa taglia**
een **kwes**to ko-**lo**ray ch**e** solo **kwes**ta **tal**-ya
In this colour we only have this size

| | |
|---|---|
| bigger | **più grande**<br>pee-**oo gran**-day |
| smaller | **più piccola**<br>pee-**oo peek**-kola |
| in other colours | **in altri colori**<br>een **al**tree ko-**lo**ree |

**YOU MAY HEAR...**

| | |
|---|---|
| **Che numero porta?**<br>kay **noo**-mayro **por**ta? | What shoe size do you take? |

# Clothes (articles)

| | | |
|---|---|---|
| blouse | **la camicetta** | kamee-**chet**-ta |
| coat | **il cappotto** | kap-**pot**-to |
| dress | **il vestito** | ves-**tee**to |
| jacket | **la giacca** | **jak**-ka |
| jumper | **la maglia** | **mal**-ya |
| knickers | **le mutandine** | mootan-**dee**nay |

| | | |
|---|---|---|
| shirt | **la camicia** | ka-**mee**cha |
| shorts | **i calzoncini corti** | kaltson-**chee**nee **kor**tee |
| skirt | **la gonna** | **gon**-na |
| socks | **i calzini** | kalt-**see**nee |
| swimsuit | **il costume da bagno** | ko-**stoo**may da **ban**-yo |
| t-shirt | **la maglietta** | mal-**yet**-ta |
| trousers | **i pantaloni** | panta-**lo**nee |

# Maps and guides

| | | |
|---|---|---|
| **l'edicola** | lay-**dee**kola | kiosk |
| **una rivista** | oona ree**vee**sta | a weekly magazine |
| **il giornale** | eel jor-**na**lay | newspaper |

Do you have a map...? **Avete una piantina...?**
a-**vay**tay oona peean-**tee**na...?

of the town **della città**
**del**-la cheet-**ta**

of the region **della regione**
**del**-la ray-**jo**nay

Can you show me where ... is on the map? **Mi può indicare dov'è ... sulla piantina?**
mee pw**o** een-dee**ka**ray do-**ve** ... **sool**-la peean-**tee**na?





> **Paying** (p 89) > **Numbers** (p 112)

| | |
|---|---|
| Do you have a guidebook/a leaflet in English? | **Avete una guida/un opuscolo in inglese?**<br>a-**vay**tay oona **gwee**da/oon o**poo**-skolo een een-**glay**zay? |
| Do you have any English newspapers/ books? | **Avete dei giornali/dei libri inglesi?**<br>a-**vay**tay day jor-**na**lee/**lee**bree een-**glay**zee? |

# Post office

Post offices are open approx. 8.30 am to 1.45 pm Mon. to Fri. (8.30 am to 12.45 pm Sat.) and sometimes until 4 pm in large towns. For a quicker service ask for **posta prioritaria** (posta pree-oree-**tar**-ya). There are special postboxes for **posta prioritaria**.

| | |
|---|---|
| **la posta** la **pos**ta | post office |
| **i francobolli** ee franko-**bol**-lee | stamps |

| | |
|---|---|
| Where is the post office? | **Scusi, dov'è la posta?**<br>**skoo**zee do-**ve** la **pos**ta? |
| When does it open? | **A che ora apre?**<br>a kay **o**ra **ap**ray? |

> **Paying** (p 89)

Which is the counter...? — **Qual è lo sportello...?**
kwal **e** lo sport-**tel**-lo...?

for stamps — **per i francobolli**
payr ee franko-**bol**-lee

for parcels — **per i pacchi**
payr ee **pak**-kee

6 stamps for postcards... — **Sei francobolli per cartoline...**
say franko-**bol**-lee payr karto-**lee**nay...

priority post — **posta prioritaria**
**pos**ta pree-oree-**tar**-ya

for Britain — **per la Gran Bretagna**
payr la gran bray**ta**nya

for America — **per gli Stati Uniti**
payr lyee **sta**tee oo**nee**tee

for Australia — **per l'Australia**
payr low-**stra**lya

**YOU MAY HEAR...**

| | |
|---|---|
| **Può comprare i francobolli dal tabaccaio**<br>pw**o** kom-**pra**ray ee franko-**bol**-lee dal tabak-**ka**-yo | You can buy stamps at the tobacconist |

# Photos

Film can be bought at photographic shops, gift shops or supermarkets, but not at pharmacies.

| | |
|---|---|
| A tape for this camcorder | **Una cassetta per questa videocamera**<br>oona kas-**set**-ta payr **kwes**ta **vee**day-o-**ka**mayra |
| Do you have batteries/ a memory card for this camera? | **Avete le pile/una scheda di memoria per questa macchina fotografica?**<br>a-**vay**tay lay **pee**lay/oona sk**ay**da dee may**mo**rya payr **kwes**ta **mak**-keena foto-**gra**-feeka? |
| Can you print these photos? | **Mi può stampare queste foto?**<br>mee pw**o** stam-**pa**-ray **kway**stay **fo**to? |

# Leisure

## Sightseeing and tourist office

The tourist office is officially called **l'Azienda di Turismo**. If you are looking for somewhere to stay, they will have details of hotels, campsites, etc. Most museums are closed on Mondays.

| | |
|---|---|
| Where is the tourist office? | **Scusi, dov'è l'ufficio turistico?**<br>**skoo**zee, do-**ve** loof-**fee**cho too-**ree**steeko? |
| What can we visit in the area? | **Che cosa c'è da vedere in questa zona?**<br>kay **ko**za ch**e** da ved-**e**ray een **kwes**ta **dzo**na? |
| in two hours | **in due ore**<br>een dooay **o**ray |
| Have you any leaflets? | **Avete degli opuscoli?**<br>a-**vay**tay **del**-yee o-**poo**skolee? |
| Are there any excursions? | **Ci sono delle gite?**<br>chee sono **del**-lay **jee**tay? |
| We'd like to go to... | **Vorremmo andare a...**<br>vor-**rem**-mo an**da**-ray a... |

| | |
|---|---|
| How much does it cost to get in? | **Quanto costa il biglietto d'entrata?** |
| | **kwan**to **kos**ta eel beel-**yet**-to den-**tra**ta? |
| Are there reductions for...? | **Ci sono riduzioni per...?** |
| | chee sono reedoots-**yo**nee payr...? |
| children | **i bambini** |
| | ee bam-**bee**nee |
| students | **gli studenti** |
| | lyee stoo-**den**tee |
| over 60s | **i pensionati** |
| | ee paynsyo**na**tee |

# Entertainment

| | |
|---|---|
| What is there to do in the evenings? | **Che cosa c'è da fare durante la sera?** |
| | kay **ko**za ch**e** da **fa**ray doo-**ran**tay la **say**ra? |
| Do you have a programme of events? | **Avete un programma degli spettacoli?** |
| | a-**vay**tay oon pro**gram**-ma **del**-yee spet-**ta**-kolee? |
| Is there anything for children? | **Ci sono spettacoli per bambini?** |
| | chee sono spet-**ta**-kolee payr bam-**bee**nee? |

> **Maps and guides** (p 66)

# Leisure/interests

| | |
|---|---|
| Where can I/ we go...? | **Dove si può andare a...?** **dov**ay see pw**o** an-**dar**ay a...? |
| fishing | **pescare** pes-**ka**ray |
| walking | **camminare** kam-mee-**na**ray |
| Are there any good beaches near here? | **Ci sono delle belle spiagge qui vicino?** chee sono **del**-lay **bel**-lay spee-**ad**-jay kwee vee-**chee**no? |
| Is there a swimming pool? | **C'è la piscina?** ch**e** la pee-**shee**na? |

# Music

| | |
|---|---|
| Are there any good concerts on? | **Ci sono dei buoni concerti?** chee sono day **bwo**nee kon-**cher**tee? |
| Where can I get tickets for the concert? | **Dove posso prendere i biglietti per il concerto?** **dov**ay **pos**-so **pren**-deray ee beel-**yet**-tee payr eel kon-**cher**to? |

Leisure

| | |
|---|---|
| Where can we hear some classical music/jazz? | **Dove possiamo sentire della musica classica/del jazz?**<br>**dov**ay pos-see-**a**mo sen-**tee**ray **del**-la **moo**-zeeka **klas**-seeka/ del jazz? |

# Cinema

| | |
|---|---|
| What's on at the cinema (name of cinema)? | **Che film danno al cinema...?**<br>kay feelm dan-no al **chee**-nayma...? |
| What time does the film start? | **A che ora comincia il film?**<br>a kay **o**ra ko-**meen**cha eel feelm? |
| How much are the tickets? | **Quanto costano i biglietti?**<br>**kwan**to **kos**tano ee beel-**yet**-tee? |
| Two for the (give time of perfomance) showing | **Due per lo spettacolo delle...**<br>dooay payr lo spet-**ta**-kolo **del**-lay... |



> **Making friends** (p 21)

# Theatre/opera

| | |
|---|---|
| **la platea** la pla**tay**a | stalls |
| **la galleria** la gal-le**reey**a | circle |
| **il loggione** eel lod-**jo**nay | upper circle |
| **il palco** eel **pal**ko | box |
| **il posto** eel **pos**to | seat |
| **il guardaroba** eel gwarda-**ro**ba | cloakroom |

| | |
|---|---|
| What is on at the theatre? | **Che cosa c'è a teatro?** kay **ko**za ch**e** a tay-**a**tro? |
| What prices are the tickets? | **Quanto costano i biglietti?** **kwan**to **kos**tano ee beel-**yet**-tee? |
| I'd like two tickets... | **Vorrei due biglietti...** vor-**ray** dooay beel-**yet**-tee... |
| for tonight | **per stasera** payr sta-**say**ra |
| for tomorrow night | **per domani sera** payr do-**ma**nee sayra |
| for the 3rd of August | **per il 3 agosto** payr il tray a**gos**to |
| When does the performance begin/end? | **A che ora comincia/finisce lo spettacolo?** a kay **o**ra ko-**meen**cha/ fee-**nee**shay lo spet-**ta**-kolo? |

Leisure

| YOU MAY HEAR... | |
|---|---|
| **Non può entrare, lo spettacolo è iniziato**<br>non pw**o** en-**tra**ray, lo spet-**ta**-kolo **e** eeneets-**ya**to | You can't go in, the performance has started |
| **Entrerà durante l'intervallo**<br>entray-**ra** doo-**ran**tay leenter-**val**-lo | You may enter at the interval |

# Television

| | |
|---|---|
| **il telecomando**<br>eel teleko-**man**do | remote control |
| **accendere** a**chen**deray | to switch on |
| **spegnere** **spen**yeray | to switch off |
| **a puntate** a poon**ta**-tay | series |
| **la telenovela**<br>la teleno**ve**la | soap |
| **il telegiornale**<br>eel telejor-**na**lay | news |
| **i cartoni animati**<br>ee kar-**to**nee anee**ma**-teechee | cartoons |

| | |
|---|---|
| Where is the television? | **Dov'è la televisione?**<br>do-**ve** la televeez-**yo**nay? |
| How do you switch it on? | **Come si accende?**<br>**ko**may see at-**chen**-day? |
| What is on television? | **Che cosa c'è alla televisione?**<br>kay **ko**za ch**e** al-la televeez-**yo**nay? |
| When is the news? | **A che ora c'è il telegiornale?**<br>a kay ora ch**e** eel telejor-**na**lay? |
| Do you have any English-language channels? | **Ci sono dei canali dove parlano in inglese?**<br>chee sono day ka**na**lee **dov**ay **par**lano een een-**glay**say? |
| Do you have any English videos? | **Avete delle videocassette in inglese?**<br>a-**vay**tay **del**-lay vee-day-o-kas-**set**-tay een een-**glay**say? |

## Sport

| | |
|---|---|
| Where can we play...? | **Dove possiamo giocare a...?**<br>**dov**ay pos-see-**a**mo jo-**ka**ray a...? |
| Where can I/we go...? | **Dove si può andare a...?**<br>**dov**ay see pw**o** an-**da**ray a...? |
| swimming | **nuotare**<br>nwo-**ta**ray |
| jogging | **fare il footing**<br>**fa**ray eel **foo**ting |

| | |
|---|---|
| Do you have to be a member? | **Si deve essere soci?**<br>see **dev**ay **es**-seray **so**chee? |
| How much is it per hour? | **Quanto costa all'ora?**<br>**kwan**to **kos**ta al**lo**ra? |
| Can we hire...? | **Si può noleggiare...?**<br>see pw**o** noled-**ja**ray...? |
| rackets | **le racchette**<br>lay rak-**ket**-tay |
| golf clubs | **le mazze da golf**<br>lay **mat**say da golf |
| We'd like to see (name team) play | **Vorremmo vedere giocare...**<br>vor-**rem**-mo ved-**er**ay jo-**ka**ray... |
| Where can I/we get tickets for the game? | **Dove si possono comprare i biglietti per la partita?**<br>**do**vay see **pos**-sono kom-**pra**ray ee beel-**yet**-tee payr la par-**tee**ta? |

| YOU MAY HEAR... | |
|---|---|
| **Non ci sono più biglietti per la partita**<br>non chee sono pyoo beel-**yet**-tee payr la par-**tee**ta | There are no tickets left for the game |

# Skiing

| | |
|---|---|
| **lo sci di fondo**<br>lo shee dee **fon**do | cross-country skiing |
| **lo skipass** lo **skee**pas | ski pass |

| | |
|---|---|
| I want to hire skis | **Vorrei noleggiare degli sci**<br>vor-**ray** noled-**ja**ray **del**-yee shee |
| Does the price include...? | **Il prezzo comprende...?**<br>eel **prets**-so kom-**pren**day...? |
| boots | **gli scarponi**<br>lee skar-**po**nee |
| poles | **le racchette**<br>lay rak-**ket**-tay |
| How much is a ... pass? | **Quanto costa lo skipass...?**<br>**kwan**to **kos**ta lo **skee**-pass...? |
| daily | **giornaliero**<br>jornal-**ye**ro |
| weekly | **settimanale**<br>set-teema-**na**lay |
| When is the last ascent? | **Quand'è l'ultima salita?**<br>kwan-**de lool**-teema sa-**lee**ta? |
| Can you adjust my bindings? | **Può regolare i miei attachi?**<br>pw**o** rego-**la**ray ee mee-**yay** at-**tak**-kee? |

| YOU MAY HEAR... | |
|---|---|
| **Ha mai sciato prima di adesso?**<br>a **ma**-ee shee-**a**to **pree**ma dee a**des**-so? | Have you ever skied before? |
| **Quale misura di sci vuole?**<br>**kwa**lay mee-**zoo**ra dee shee **vwo**lay? | What length skis do you want? |
| **Quale numero di scarponi porta?**<br>**kwa**lay **noo**-mayro dee skar-**po**nee **por**ta? | What is your boot size? |
| **Vuole lezioni di sci?**<br>**vwo**lay lets-**ee**onee dee shee? | Do you want skiing lessons? |

# Walking

| | |
|---|---|
| Are there any guided walks? | **Ci sono dei percorsi guidati?**<br>chee sono day per**kor**see gwee-**da**tee? |
| Do you know any good walks? | **Ci può consigliare un buon percorso?**<br>chee pw**o** konseel-**ya**ray oon bwon per**kor**so? |

| | |
|---|---|
| How many kilometres is the walk? | **Di quanti chilometri è il percorso?** |
| | dee **kwan**tee kee**lo**-metree **e** eel per**kor**so? |
| Is it very steep? | **È molto in salita?** |
| | **e mol**to een sa-**lee**ta? |
| How long will it take? | **Quanto ci vorrà?** |
| | **kwan**to chee vor-**ra**? |
| Is there a map of the walk? | **C'è la piantina del percorso?** |
| | ch**e** la peean-**tee**na del per**kor**so? |
| We'd like to go climbing | **Vorremmo andare a fare una scalata** |
| | vor-**rem**-mo an-**da**ray a **fa**ray oona ska**la**ta |
| Do you have a detailed map of the area? | **Avete una piantina dettagliata della zona?** |
| | a-**vay**tay oona peean-**tee**na det-tal-**ya**ta **del**-la **dzo**na? |





> **Maps and guides** (p 66)

# Communications

## Telephone and mobile

The international code for Italy is **00 39** plus the Italian town or area code less the first **0**. If you are calling the UK from abroad, the UK international code is **00 44** plus the area code less the first **0**. If you are calling within Italy, you must always use the full area code, even for local calls.

| | |
|---|---|
| **la scheda telefonica**<br>la **skay**da tele-**fo**neeka | phonecard |
| **il telefonino**<br>eel telefo-**nee**no | mobile |
| **la cellulare**<br>la chel-loo-**la**ray | mobile |

I want to make a phone call — **Vorrei fare una telefonata**
vor-**ray fa**ray oona telefo-**na**ta

Where can I buy a phonecard? — **Dove posso comprare una scheda telefonica?**
**do**vay **pos**-so kom-**pra**ray oona **skay**da tele-**fo**neeka?

| | |
|---|---|
| A phonecard for ... euros | **Una scheda telefonica da ... euro**<br>oona **skay**da tele-**fo**neeka da ... ay-**oo**-ro |
| Do you have a mobile? | **Ha il telefonino?**<br>a eel telefo-**nee**no? |
| What is the number of your mobile? | **Qual è il numero del suo telefonino?**<br>kwal **e** eel **noo**-mayro del **soo**-o telefo-**nee**no? |
| My mobile number is... | **Il numero del mio telefonino è...**<br>eel **noo**-mayro del **mee**yo telefo-**nee**no **e**... |
| Mr Bruni, please | **Il Signor Bruni per favore**<br>eel seen-**yor** Brunee payr fa-**vo**ray |
| extension... | **interno...**<br>eenter**er**no... |

Communications

**FACE TO FACE**

A **Pronto**
**pron**to
Hello

B **Vorrei parlare con..., per favore**
**vor**-ray par**la**ray kon..., payr fa-**vo**ray
I'd like to speak to..., please

A **Chi parla?**
kee **par**la?
Who's calling?

B **Sono Angela**
**so**no Angela
It's Angela

A **Un momento...**
oon mo-**men**to...
Just a moment...

| | |
|---|---|
| Can I speak to...? | **Posso parlare con...?** pos-so parlaray kon...? |
| I'll call back later | **Richiamo più tardi** reekee-**a**mo pyoo **tar**dee |
| I'll call back tomorrow | **Richiamo domani** reekee-**a**mo do-**ma**nee |
| This is Mr.../Mrs... | **Sono il Signor.../la Signora...** **so**no eel seen-**yor**.../ la seen-**yo**ra... |

**YOU MAY HEAR...**

| | |
|---|---|
| **La sto mettendo in linea** la sto met-**ten**do een **lee**nay-a | I'm trying to connect you |
| **La linea è occupata** la **lee**nay-a **e** ok-koo-**pa**ta | The line is engaged |

Telephone and mobile

| YOU MAY HEAR... | |
|---|---|
| **Provi più tardi**<br>**pro**vee pyoo **tar**dee | Please try later |
| **Vuole lasciare un messaggio?**<br>**vwo**lay la-**sha**ray oon mes-**sad**-jo? | Do you want to leave a message? |
| **...lasciate un messaggio dopo il segnale acustico**<br>...la-**sha**tay oon mes-**sad**-jo **do**po eel sen-**ya**lay a-**koo**-steeko | ...leave a message after the tone |
| **Per favore spegnete i telefonini**<br>payr fa-**vo**ray spen-**yay**tay ee telefo-**nee**nee | Please switch off all mobile phones |

## Text messaging

| | |
|---|---|
| I will text you | **Ti mando un messaggio**<br>tee **man**do oon mes-**sad**-jo |
| Can you text me? | **Può mandarmi un messaggio?**<br>pwo man**dar**mee oon mes-**sad**-jo? |

# E-mail

An informal way of addressing an e-mail is **Ciao...** and ending it with **a presto** (speak to you soon). For more formal e-mails, begin either **Caro...** (for a man) or **Cara...** (for a woman).

| | |
|---|---|
| **Nuovo messaggio** | New message |
| **A** | To |
| **Da** | From |
| **Oggetto** | Subject |
| **Cc** | cc |
| **Ccn** | bcc |
| **Allegato** | Attachment |
| **Invio** | Send |

| | |
|---|---|
| Do you have e-mail? | **Ha un indirizzo e-mail?**<br>a oon eendee-**reet**-so e-mail? |
| What is your e-mail address? | **Qual è il suo indirizzo e-mail?**<br>kwal e eel **soo**-o eendee-**reet**-so e-mail? |
| How do you spell it? | **Come si scrive?**<br>**ko**may see **skree**vay? |
| All one word | **Tutta una parola**<br>**toot**-ta oona pa-**ro**la |
| All lower case | **Lettere minuscole**<br>let-**te**ray mee-**noos**kolay |

E-mail

| | |
|---|---|
| My e-mail address is... | **Il mio indirizzo e-mail è...**<br>eel **mee**-yo eendee-**reet**-so e-mail e... |
| clare.smith@ bit.co.uk | **clare punto smith chiocciola bit punto chee oh punto oo kappa**<br>clare **poon**to smith kee-**yo**chola bit **poon**to chee oh **poon**to oo **kap**-pa |
| Can I send an e-mail? | **Posso mandare un'e-mail?**<br>**pos**-so man-**da**ray oon e-mail? |
| Did you get my e-mail? | **Ha ricevuto la mia e-mail?**<br>**a** reechay-**voo**to la **mee**ya e-mail? |



# Internet

Most computer terminology tends to be in English and you find the same with the internet.

| | |
|---|---|
| Are there any internet cafés here? | **Ci sono degli internet café qui vicino?**<br>chee sono **del**-yee **een**ternet ka**fay** kwee vee-**chee**no? |
| How much is it to log on for an hour? | **Quanto costa un'ora in internet?**<br>**kwan**to **kos**ta oon **o**ra een **een**ternet? |

# Fax

The code to send faxes to Italy from the UK is **00 39** plus the Italian area code without the first **0**. The code to fax the UK from Italy is **00 44**.

## Addressing a fax

| | |
|---|---|
| **a** | to |
| **da** | from |
| **data** | date |
| **oggetto**: | re: |
| **le invio** | please find attached |
| **una copia di...** | a copy of... |
| **...pagine in totale** | ...pages in total |

| | |
|---|---|
| Do you have a fax? | **Avete un fax?**<br>a-**vay**tay oon fax? |
| I want to send a fax | **Vorrei mandare un fax**<br>vor-**ray** man-**da**ray oon fax |
| What is your fax number? | **Qual è il suo numero di fax?**<br>kwal **e** eel **soo**-o **noo**-mayro dee fax? |
| My fax number is... | **Il mio numero di fax è...**<br>eel **mee**yo **noo**-mayro dee fax **e**... |

# Practicalities

## Money

Banks are open approx. 8.30 am to 1.30 pm Mon. to Fri. (and sometimes also 3 to 4 pm). The euro is the currency of Italy. Euro cents are known as **centesimi** (chen-**tay**-zeemee).

| | |
|---|---|
| **la carta di credito**<br>la karta dee **kray**-deeto | credit card |
| **il bancomat**<br>eel **ban**komat | cash dispenser |
| **lo scontrino**<br>lo skon-**tree**no | till receipt |

| | |
|---|---|
| Where can I change some money? | **Dove posso cambiare i soldi?**<br>**do**vay **pos**-so kamb-**ya**ray ee **sol**dee? |
| When does the bank open? | **Quando apre la banca?**<br>**kwan**do **a**pray la **ban**ka? |
| When does the bank close? | **Quando chiude la banca?**<br>**kwan**do kee-**oo**day la **ban**ka? |

| | |
|---|---|
| Can I pay with...? | **Posso pagare con...?**<br>**pos**-so pa-**ga**ray kon...? |
| euros | **euro**<br>ay-**oo**-ro |
| Swiss francs | **franchi svizzeri**<br>**fran**kee **zveet**-seree |
| I want to change these traveller's cheques | **Vorrei cambiare questi traveller's cheques**<br>vor-**ray** kamb-**ya**ray **kwes**tee travellers cheques |
| Where is the nearest cash dispenser? | **Dov'è il bancomat più vicino?**<br>do-**ve** eel **ban**komat pyoo vee-**chee**no? |
| Can I use my credit card at the cash dispenser? | **Posso usare la mia carta di credito al bancomat?**<br>**pos**-so oo-**za**ray la **mee**ya **kar**ta dee **kray**-deeto al **ban**komat? |
| Do you have any small change? | **Scusi, ha spiccioli?**<br>**skoo**zee, a **speet**-cholee? |

# Paying

In Italy it is illegal to leave a shop, bar, etc., without a receipt.

| | |
|---|---|
| How much is it? | **Quanto costa?**<br>**kwan**to **kos**ta? |

| | |
|---|---|
| How much will it be? | **Quanto costerà?** |
| | **kwan**to **kos**tay-**ra**? |
| Can I pay by...? | **Posso pagare con...?** |
| | **pos**-so pa-**ga**ray kon...? |
| credit card | **la carta di credito** |
| | la **kar**ta dee **kray**-deeto |
| cheque | **un assegno** |
| | oon as-**sen**-yo |
| Is service included? | **il servizio è compreso?** |
| | eel ser**veets**-yo **e** kom-**pray**zo? |
| Is tax included? | **l'IVA è compresa?** |
| | leeva e kom-**pray**za? |
| Put it on my bill | **Lo metta sul mio conto** |
| | lo **met**-ta sool **mee**yo **kon**to |
| Where do I pay? | **Dove devo pagare?** |
| | **do**vay **de**vo pa-**ga**ray? |
| I need a receipt, please | **Ho bisogno di una ricevuta, per favore** |
| | o bee**zon**-yo dee oona reechay-**voo**ta, payr fa-**vo**ray |
| Do I pay in advance? | **Devo pagare in anticipo?** |
| | **de**vo pa-**ga**ray een an**tee**-cheepo? |
| Do I need to pay a deposit? | **Devo dare una caparra?** |
| | **de**vo **da**ray oona ka**par**-ra? |
| I'm sorry | **Mi dispiace** |
| | mee deespee-**a**-chay |
| I've nothing smaller (no change) | **Non ho spiccioli** |
| | non **o speet**-cholee |

Practicalities

| YOU MAY HEAR... | |
|---|---|
| **L'iva è compresa**<br>leeva **e** kom-**pray**za | VAT is included |
| **Il servizio è incluso ma non la mancia**<br>eel ser**veets**-yo **e** een-**kloo**so ma non la **man**cha | Service is included but not a tip |
| **Paghi alla cassa**<br>**pa**gee **al**-la **kas**-sa | Pay at the till |
| **Prima ritiri lo scontrino alla cassa** (at airport, station bars, etc.)<br>**pree**ma ree**tee**-ree lo skon-**tree**no **al**-la **kas**-sa | First get a receipt/ chit at the till |

# Luggage

| | |
|---|---|
| **il ritiro bagagli**<br>eel ree**tee**ro ba-**ga**lyee | baggage reclaim |
| **il deposito bagagli**<br>eel day-**po**zeeto ba-**ga**lyee | left-luggage office |
| **il carrello** eel kar-**rel**-lo | luggage trolley |

My luggage hasn't arrived — **Il mio bagaglio non è arrivato**
eel **mee**yo ba**gal**-yo non **e** ar-ree**va**to

My suitcase has been damaged on the flight | **La mia valigia è stata danneggiata durante il volo**
la **mee**ya va-**lee**ja **e sta**ta dan-ned-**ja**ta doo-**ran**tay eel **vo**lo

## Repairs

| | |
|---|---|
| This is broken. Where can I have it repaired? | **Questo è rotto. Dove posso farlo riparare?**<br>**kwes**to **e rot**-to. **dov**ay **pos**-so **far**-lo reepa-**ra**ray? |
| Is it worth repairing? | **Vale la pena di ripararlo?**<br>**va**lay la **pay**na dee reepa-**rar**lo? |
| Can you repair...? | **Può riparare...?**<br>pw**o** reepa-**ra**ray...? |
| this | **questo**<br>**kwes**to |
| these shoes | **queste scarpe**<br>**kwes**tay **skar**pay |
| my watch | **il mio orologio**<br>eel **mee**yo oro-**lo**jo |

**YOU MAY HEAR...**

| | |
|---|---|
| **Mi dispiace ma non si può riparare**<br>mee deespee-**a**-chay ma non see pw**o** reepa-**ra**ray | Sorry, but we can't mend it |

Practicalities



**Breakdown** (p47)

# Complaints

| | |
|---|---|
| This does not work | **Questo non funziona**<br>**kwes**to non foonts-**yo**na |
| It's dirty | **È sporco(a)**<br>e **spor**ko(a) |
| The ... does not work | **Il/La/Lo ... non funziona**<br>eel/la/lo ... non foonts-**yo**na |
| The ... do not work | **I/Le/Gli ... non funzionano**<br>ee/lay/lyee ... non foonts-**yo**nano |
| light | **la luce**<br>la **loo**chay |
| toilet | **il bagno**<br>eel **ban**-yo |
| heating | **il riscaldamento**<br>eel reeskalda-**men**to |
| air conditioning | **l'aria condizionata**<br>**la**rya kondeetsyo-**na**ta |
| It's broken | **È rotto(a)**<br>**e rot**-to(a) |
| I want a refund | **Vorrei un rimborso**<br>vor-**ray** oon reem-**bor**so |



> **Hotel desk** (p 54)

# Problems

Can you help me? **Può aiutarmi?**
pw**o** a-yoo-**tar**mee?

I speak very little Italian **Parlo molto poco l'italiano**
**par**lo **mol**to **po**ko leetal-**ya**no

Does anyone here speak English? **C'è qualcuno che parla inglese?**
ch**e** kwal-**koo**no kay **par**la een-**glay**say?

What's the matter? **Che cosa c'è?**
kay **ko**za ch**e**?

I would like to speak to whoever is in charge of... **Vorrei parlare con chi è incaricato di...**
vor-**ray** par-**la**ray kon kee **e** eenkaree-**ka**to dee...

I'm lost **Mi sono smarrito(a)**
mee sono smar-**ree**to(a)

How do you get to... **Come si fa per andare a...**
**ko**may see fa payr an-**da**ray a...

I missed my train/plane/connection **Ho perso il treno/l'aereo/la coincidenza**
o **per**so eel **tray**no/la-**ayr**ay-o/la koeenchee-**den**tsa

I've missed my flight because there was a strike **Ho perso l'aereo perché c'era lo sciopero**
o **per**so la-**ayr**ay-o per-**ke** chera lo **sho**-pero

Practicalities

| | |
|---|---|
| The coach has left without me | **Il pullman è partito senza di me** |
| | eel **pool**man **e** par-**tee**-to **sen**tsa dee may |
| Can you show me how this works, please? | **Mi fa vedere come funziona per favore?** |
| | mee fa vay-**de**ray **ko**may foonts-**yo**na payr fa-**vo**ray? |
| I have lost my money | **Ho perso i miei soldi** |
| | o **per**so ee mee-**yay sol**dee |
| I need to get to... | **Devo andare a...** |
| | **de**vo an-**da**ray a... |
| I need to get in touch with the British consulate | **Devo contattare il consolato britannico** |
| | **de**vo kontat-**ta**ray eel konso-**la**to bree**tan**-neeko |
| Leave me alone! | **Mi lasci in pace!** |
| | mee **lash**-ee een **pa**-chay! |
| Go away! | **Se ne vada!** |
| | say nay **va**da! |



> **Hotel desk** (p 54)

# Emergencies

| | |
|---|---|
| **l'ambulanza**<br>lamboo-**lan**tsa | ambulance |
| **i carabinieri**<br>ee karabeen-**ye**ree | military police |
| **la polizia** la poleet-**see**-a | police |
| **i pompieri**<br>ee pomp-**ye**ree | fire fighters |
| **i vigili del fuoco**<br>ee **veed**-jeelay del **fwo**ko | fire brigade |
| **il commissariato**<br>eel kom-mees-ar**ya**to | police station |
| **la questura**<br>la kwes-**too**ra | police station |

Help! — **Aiuto!**
a-**yoo**to!

Fire! — **Fuoco!**
**fwo**ko!

Can you help me? — **Può aiutarmi?**
pw**o** a-yoo-**tar**mee?

There's been an accident! — **C'è stato un incidente!**
ch**e** stato oon eenchee-**den**tay!

Someone... — **Qualcuno...**
kwal-**koo**no...

has been injured — **si è fatto male**
see **e fat**-to **ma**lay

| | |
|---|---|
| has been knocked down | **è stato investito**<br>**e** stato eenves-**tee**to |
| Please call... | **Per favore chiami...**<br>payr fa-**vo**ray kee-**a**-mee... |
| the police | **la polizia**<br>la poleet-**see**-a |
| an ambulance | **l'ambulanza**<br>lamboo-**lan**tsa |
| Where is the police station? | **Dov'è la questura?**<br>do-**ve** la kwes-**too**ra? |
| I want to report a crime | **Vorrei denunciare un delitto**<br>vor-**ray** denoon-**cha**ray oon day-**lee**to |
| I've been... | **Mi hanno...**<br>mee **an**-no... |
| robbed | **derubato(a)**<br>deroo-**ba**to(a) |
| attacked | **assalito(a)**<br>as-sa**lee**to(a) |
| Someone's stolen... | **Mi hanno rubato...**<br>mee **an**-no roo-**ba**to... |
| my bag | **la borsa**<br>la **bor**sa |
| traveller's cheques | **i miei traveller's cheques**<br>ee mee-**yay** travellers cheques |
| My car has been broken into | **Hanno svaligiato la mia macchina**<br>**an**-no svalee-**ja**to la **mee**ya **mak**-keena |

| | |
|---|---|
| My car has been stolen | **Mi hanno rubato la macchina**<br>mee **an**-no roo-**ba**to la **mak**-keena |
| I've been raped | **Mi hanno violentata**<br>mee **an**-no veeolen-**ta**ta |
| I want to speak to a policewoman | **Vorrei parlare con una agente della polizia**<br>vor-**ray** par-**lar**ay kon oona a-**jen**tay **del**-la poleet-**see**-a |
| I need to make a telephone call | **Devo fare una telefonata**<br>**de**vo **fa**ray oona telefo-**na**ta |
| I need a report for my insurance | **Ho bisogno di un verbale per la mia assicurazione**<br>o bee**zon**-yo dee oon ver-**ba**lay payr la **mee**ya as-seekoorats-**yo**nay |
| I didn't know there was a speed limit | **Non sapevo che c'era il limite di velocità**<br>non sa-**pay**vo kay **che**ra eel **lee**-meetay dee velochee-**ta** |
| How much is the fine? | **Quant'è la multa?**<br>kwan-**te** la **mool**ta? |
| Where do I pay it? | **Dove pago?**<br>**do**vay **pa**go? |
| Do I have to pay it straight away? | **Devo pagarla subito?**<br>**de**vo pa-**gar**la **soo**-beeto? |
| I'm very sorry, officer | **Mi dispiace, signor agente**<br>mee deespee-**a**-chay, seen-**yor** a-**jen**tay |

Practicalities

# Health

## Pharmacy

| | |
|---|---|
| **la farmacia**<br>la farma-**chee**ya | pharmacy/chemist |
| **la farmacia di turno**<br>la farma-**chee**ya dee **toor**no | duty chemist |

| | |
|---|---|
| Can you give me something for...? | **Mi dà qualcosa contro il/ la** (etc.)**...?**<br>mee **da** kwal-**ko**za **kon**tro eel/la...? |
| a headache | **il mal di testa**<br>eel mal dee **tes**ta |
| car sickness | **il mal d'auto**<br>eel mal **dow**to |
| a cough | **la tosse**<br>la **tos**-say |
| diarrhoea | **la diarrea**<br>la deear-**ray**-a |
| Is it safe for children? | **Va bene per bambini?**<br>va **be**nay payr bam-**bee**nee? |
| How much should I give him? | **Quanto gliene devo dare?**<br>**kwan**to lyee-**ay**-nay **de**vo **da**ray? |

| YOU MAY HEAR... | |
|---|---|
| **Tre volte al giorno...**<br>tray **vol**tay al **jor**no... | Three times a day... |
| **prima**<br>**pree**ma | before |
| **con**<br>kon | with |
| **dopo**<br>**do**po | after |
| **...i pasti**<br>...ee **pas**tee | ...meals |

# Doctor

In Italian the possessive (my, his, her, etc.) is generally not used with parts of the body, e.g.

I've broken my leg **Ho rotto la gamba**
He's hurt his foot **Si è fatto male al piede**

| | |
|---|---|
| **ospedale** ospay-**da**lay | hospital |
| **pronto soccorso** **pron**to sok-**kor**so | casualty |
| **USL** **oo**sel | local health centre |

**FACE TO FACE**

**A** **Mi sento male**
mee **sen**to **ma**lay
I feel ill

**B** **Ha la febbre?**
a la **feb**-bray?
Do you have a temperature?

**A** **No. Ho un dolore qui...**
No. o oon do-**lo**ray kwee...
No. I have a pain here...

| | |
|---|---|
| I need a doctor | **Ho bisogno di un medico**<br>o bee**zon**-yo dee oon **med**-eeko |
| My son is ill | **Mio figlio è malato**<br>**mee**yo **feel**-yo **e** ma-**la**to |
| My daughter is ill | **Mia figlia è malata**<br>**mee**ya **feel**-ya **e** ma-**la**ta |
| I'm diabetic | **Sono diabetico(a)**<br>sono deea-**be**-teeko(a) |
| I'm pregnant | **Sono incinta**<br>sono een**cheen**-ta |
| I'm on the pill | **Prendo la pillola**<br>prendo la **peel**-lola |
| I'm allergic to penicillin | **Sono allergico(a) alla penicillina**<br>sono al-**ler**-jeeko(a) al-la penee-cheel-**lee**na |

| | |
|---|---|
| Will he/she have to go to hospital? | **Deve andare all'ospedale?**<br>**de**vay an-**da**ray al-lospay-**da**lay? |
| When are visiting hours? | **Qual è l'orario di visita?**<br>kwal **e** lo**rar**-yo dee **vee**-zeeta? |
| Will I have to pay? | **Dovrò pagare?**<br>dov-**ro** pa-**ga**ray? |
| How much will it cost? | **Quanto costerà?**<br>**kwan**to kostay-**ra**? |
| Can you give me a receipt for the insurance? | **Mi dà la ricevuta per l'assicurazione?**<br>mee **da** la reechay-**voo**ta payr las-seekoorats-**yo**nay? |

| YOU MAY HEAR... | |
|---|---|
| **Deve andare all'ospedale**<br>**de**vay an-**da**ray al-lospay-**da**lay | You will have to go to hospital |
| **Non è grave**<br>non **e gra**vay | It's not serious |




> **Emergencies** (p 96)

# Dentist

| | |
|---|---|
| I need a dentist | **Ho bisogno di un dentista**<br>o bee**zon**-yo dee oon den-**tees**ta |
| He/She has toothache | **Ha mal di denti**<br>a mal dee **den**tee |
| Can you do a temporary filling? | **Può fare un'otturazione provvisoria?**<br>pw**o** faray oonot-toorats-**yo**nay prov-vee-**so**ree-a? |
| It hurts | **Fa male**<br>fa **ma**lay |
| Can you give me something for the pain? | **Può darmi qualcosa per calmare il dolore?**<br>pw**o** **dar**mee kwal-**ko**za payr kal**ma**ray eel do-**lo**ray? |
| Can you repair my dentures? | **Può riparare la mia dentiera?**<br>pw**o** reepa-**ra**ray la **mee**ya dent-**ye**ra? |
| Do I have to pay? | **Devo pagare?**<br>**de**vo pa-**ga**ray? |
| How much will it be? | **Quanto costerà?**<br>**kwan**to kostay-**ra**? |
| Can I have a receipt for my insurance? | **Mi dà la ricevuta per la mia assicurazione?**<br>mee **da** la reechay-**voo**ta payr la **mee**ya as-seekoorats-**yo**nay? |

| YOU MAY HEAR... | |
|---|---|
| **Devo fare un'estrazione** **de**vo **fa**ray oones-trats-**yo**nay | I'll have to take it out |
| **Le occorre un'otturazione** lay o-**kor**-ray oonot-toorats-**yo**nay | You need a filling |
| **Questo le potrà fare un po' male** **kwes**to lay po-**tra** **fa**ray oon po **ma**lay | This might hurt a little |

# Different types of travellers

## Disabled travellers

| | |
|---|---|
| What facilities do you have for disabled people? | **Quali servizi avete per i disabili?** <br> **kwa**lee ser**veets**-ee a-**vay**tay payr ee dee-**za**beelee? |
| Are there any toilets for the disabled? | **Ci sono le toilette per i disabili?** <br> chee sono le twa**let** payr ee dee-**za**beelee? |
| Do you have any bedrooms on the ground floor? | **Avete delle camere al pianterreno?** <br> a-**vay**tay **del**-lay **ka**-mayray al pyan-ter-**ray**no? |
| Is there a lift? | **C'è l'ascensore?** <br> **che** lashen-**so**ray? |
| Where is the lift? | **Dov'è l'ascensore?** <br> do-**ve** lashen-**so**ray? |
| Can you visit ... in a wheelchair? | **Si può visitare ... nella sedia a rotelle?** <br> see pw**o** vee-zee-**ta**ray ... **nay**-la **sed**-ya a ro**tel**-lay? |

| | |
|---|---|
| Do you have wheelchairs? | **Avete delle sedie a rotelle?** a-**vay**tay **del**-lay **sed**-yay a ro**tel**-lay? |
| Where is the wheelchair-accessible entrance? | **Dov'è l'accesso per la sedia a rotelle?** do-**ve** lat-**ches**-so payr la **sed**-ya a ro**tel**-lay? |
| Do you have an induction loop? | **Avete un auricolare?** a-**vay**tay oon owree-ko-**la**ray? |
| Is there a reduction for disabled people? | **C'è una riduzione per i disabili?** **che** oona reedoots-**yo**nay payr ee dee-**za**beelee? |
| Is there somewhere I can sit down? | **Scusi, dove posso sedermi?** **skoo**zee **do**vay **pos**-so sed-**er**mee? |

# With kids

Public transport is free for children under 4. Children between 4 and 12 pay half price.

| | |
|---|---|
| A child's ticket | **Un biglietto per bambini** oon beel-**yet**-to payr bam-**bee**nee |
| He/She is ... years old | **Ha ... anni** a ... **an**-nee |





> **Hotel** (p 52)

| | |
|---|---|
| Is there a reduction for children? | **C'è la riduzione per bambini?**<br>che la ree-doots-**yo**nay payr bam-**bee**nee? |
| Do you have a children's menu? | **Avete il menù per bambini?**<br>a-**vay**tay eel me**noo** payr bam-**bee**nee? |
| Is it OK to take children? | **Si possono portare i bambini?**<br>see **pos**-sono por-**ta**ray ee bam-**bee**nee? |
| Do you have...? | **Avete...?**<br>a-**vay**tay...? |
| a high chair | **un seggiolone**<br>oon sed-jo**lo**-nay |
| a cot | **un lettino**<br>oon let-**tee**no |
| I have two children | **Ho due figli**<br>o dooay **feel**-yee |
| He/She is 8 years old | **Ha otto anni**<br>a **ot**-to **an**-nee |
| Do you have any children? | **Ha figli?**<br>a **feel**-yee? |

With kids

> **Pharmacy** (p 99) > **Doctor** (p 100)

# Reference

## Alphabet

J, K, W, X and Y are not native to the Italian language. You will only see these letters in foreign words. Below are the words used for clarification when spelling something out.

| | |
|---|---|
| **Come si scrive?**<br>komay see **skree**vay? | How do you spell it? |
| **A come Ancona,**<br>**B come Bari**<br>a komay an-**ko**na,<br>bee komay **ba**-ree | A for Ancona,<br>B for Bari |

| | | | |
|---|---|---|---|
| **A** | a | **Ancona** | an-**ko**na |
| **B** | bee | **Bari** | **ba**-ree |
| **C** | chee | **Como** | **ko**mo |
| **D** | dee | **Domodossola** | domo-**dos**-sola |
| **E** | ay | **Empoli** | **em**-polee |
| **F** | **ef**-fe | **Firenze** | fee-**ren**tsay |
| **G** | jee | **Genova** | **je**-nova |
| **H** | **ak**-ka | **Hotel** | **o**-tel |

| | | | |
|---|---|---|---|
| **I** | ee | **Imola** | **ee**-mola |
| **L** | **el**-le | **Livorno** | lee-**vor**no |
| **M** | **em**-me | **Milano** | mee-**la**no |
| **N** | **en**-ne | **Napoli** | **na**-polee |
| **O** | o | **Otranto** | **o**-tranto |
| **P** | pee | **Palermo** | pa-**layr**mo |
| **Q** | koo | **Quarto** | **kwar**-to |
| **R** | **er**-re | **Roma** | **ro**-ma |
| **S** | **es**-se | **Savona** | sa-**vo**na |
| **T** | tee | **Torino** | to-**ree**no |
| **U** | oo | **Udine** | **oo**-deenay |
| **V** | voo | **Venezia** | ve**net**seeya |
| **Z** | **dze**-ta | **Zara** | **dza**ra |
| **J** | ee **loon**-ga | | |
| **K** | **kap**-pa | | |
| **W** | **dop**-pyo voo | | |
| **X** | eex | | |
| **Y** | ee **gre**-ka | | |

# Measurements and quantities

1 lb = approx. 0.5 kilo 1 pint = approx. 0.5 litre

## Liquids

| | |
|---|---|
| 1/2 litre of... | **mezzo litro di...**<br>**medz**-zo **lee**tro dee... |
| a litre of... | **un litro di...**<br>oon **lee**tro dee... |
| 1/2 bottle of... | **mezza bottiglia di...**<br>**medz**-za bot-**teel**-ya dee... |
| a bottle of... | **una bottiglia di...**<br>oona bot-**teel**-ya dee... |
| a glass of... | **un bicchiere di...**<br>oon beek-**ye**ray dee... |

## Weights

| | |
|---|---|
| 100 grams | **100 grammi/un etto**<br>**chen**to **gram**-mee/oon **et**-to |
| 1/2 kilo of... | **mezzo chilo di...**<br>**medz**-zo **kee**lo dee... |
| a kilo of... | **un chilo di...**<br>oon **kee**lo dee... |

## Food

| | |
|---|---|
| a slice of... | **una fetta di...**<br>oona **fet**-ta dee... |
| a portion of... | **una porzione di...**<br>oona ports-**yo**nay dee... |

Reference

| | |
|---|---|
| a dozen... | **una dozzina di...**<br>oona dodz-**zee**na dee... |
| a box of... | **una scatola di...**<br>oona **ska**-tola dee... |
| a packet of... | **un pacchetto di...**<br>oon pak-**ket**-to dee... |
| a tin of... | **una scatola di...**<br>oona **ska**-tola dee... |
| a can of...(beer) | **una lattina di...**<br>oona lat-**tee**na dee... |
| a jar of... | **un vasetto di...**<br>oon va**zet**-to dee... |

## Miscellaneous

| | |
|---|---|
| ...euros worth of... | **...euro di...**<br>...ay-**oo**-ro dee... |
| a quarter | **un quarto**<br>oon **kwar**to |
| 20 per cent | **il venti per cento**<br>eel **ven**tee payr **chen**to |
| more than... | **più di...**<br>pyoo dee... |
| less than... | **meno di...**<br>**me**no dee... |
| double | **il doppio**<br>eel **dop**-pyo |
| twice | **due volte**<br>**doo**-ay **vol**tay |

# Numbers

| | |
|---|---|
| 0 | **zero dze**-ro |
| 1 | **uno oo**no |
| 2 | **due doo**-ay |
| 3 | **tre** tray |
| 4 | **quattro kwat**-tro |
| 5 | **cinque cheen**-kway |
| 6 | **sei** say |
| 7 | **sette set**-tay |
| 8 | **otto ot**-to |
| 9 | **nove no**vay |
| 10 | **dieci** dee-**e**-chee |
| 11 | **undici oon**-deechee |
| 12 | **dodici do**-deechee |
| 13 | **tredici tray**-deechee |
| 14 | **quattordici** kwat-**tor**-deechee |
| 15 | **quindici kween**-deechee |
| 16 | **sedici say**-deechee |
| 17 | **diciasette** deechas-**set**-tay |
| 18 | **diciotto** dee**chot**-to |
| 19 | **diciannove** deechan-**no**vay |
| 20 | **venti ven**tee |
| 21 | **ventuno** ven-**too**no |
| 22 | **ventidue** ventee-**doo**-ay |
| 23 | **ventitré** ventee-**tray** |
| 24 | **ventiquattro** ventee-**kwat**-tro |

Reference

| | |
|---|---|
| 25 | **venticinque** ventee-**cheen**-kway |
| 26 | **ventisei** ventee-**say** |
| 27 | **ventisette** ventee-**set**-tay |
| 28 | **ventotto** vent-**ot**-to |
| 29 | **ventinove** ventee-**no**-vay |
| 30 | **trenta** **trayn**-ta |
| 40 | **quaranta** kwa**ran**-ta |
| 50 | **cinquanta** cheen**kwan**-ta |
| 60 | **sessanta** ses-**san**ta |
| 70 | **settanta** set-**tan**ta |
| 80 | **ottanta** ot-**tan**ta |
| 90 | **novanta** no-**van**ta |
| 100 | **cento** **chen**to |
| 110 | **cento dieci** **chen**to dee-**e**-chee |
| 1000 | **mille** meel-lay |
| 2000 | **duemila** dooay-**mee**la |
| million | **un milione** oon meel-**yo**nay |
| billion | **un miliardo** oon meel-**yar**do |

| | | | |
|---|---|---|---|
| 1st | **primo**<br>**pree**mo | 6th | **sesto**<br>**ses**to |
| 2nd | **secondo**<br>se**kon**-do | 7th | **settimo**<br>**set**-teemo |
| 3rd | **terzo**<br>**ter**tso | 8th | **ottavo**<br>ot-**ta**vo |
| 4th | **quarto**<br>**kwar**to | 9th | **nono**<br>**no**no |
| 5th | **quinto**<br>**kween**to | 10th | **decimo**<br>**de**chee-mo |

# Days and months

## Days

| | | |
|---|---|---|
| Monday | **lunedì** | loone**dee** |
| Tuesday | **martedì** | marte**dee** |
| Wednesday | **mercoledì** | merkole**dee** |
| Thursday | **giovedì** | jove**dee** |
| Friday | **venerdì** | vener**dee** |
| Saturday | **sabato** | **sa**-bato |
| Sunday | **domenica** | do**me**neeka |

## Months

| | | |
|---|---|---|
| January | **gennaio** | jen-**na**-yo |
| February | **febbraio** | feb-**ra**-yo |
| March | **marzo** | **mar**tso |
| April | **aprile** | a-**pree**lay |
| May | **maggio** | **mad**-jo |
| June | **giugno** | **joon**-yo |
| July | **luglio** | **lool**-yo |
| August | **agosto** | a-**gos**to |
| September | **settembre** | set-**tem**bray |
| October | **ottobre** | ot-**to**bray |
| November | **novembre** | nov-**em**bray |
| December | **dicembre** | dee**chem**bray |

## Seasons

| | | |
|---|---|---|
| spring | **primavera** | preema**ve**ra |
| summer | **estate** | es-**ta**tay |
| autumn | **autunno** | ow**too**no |
| winter | **inverno** | een**ver**no |

| | |
|---|---|
| What's today's date? | **Qual è la data di oggi?**<br>kwal **e** la **da**ta dee **od**jee? |
| What day is it today? | **Che giorno è oggi?**<br>kay **jor**no **e od**jee? |
| It's the 5th of March 2007 | **È il cinque marzo duemilasette**<br>**e** eel **cheen**-kway **mar**tso oo-ay-**mee**la-**sayt**-tay |
| on Saturday | **il sabato**<br>eel **sa**-bato |
| on Saturdays | **tutti i sabati**<br>**toot**-tee ee **sa**-batee |
| every Saturday | **ogni sabato**<br>**on**-yee **sa**-bato |
| this Saturday | **questo sabato**<br>**kwes**to **sa**-bato |
| next Saturday | **sabato prossimo**<br>**sa**-bato **pros**-seemo |
| last Saturday | **sabato scorso**<br>**sa**-bato **skor**so |
| in June | **a giugno**<br>a **joon**-yo |

| | |
|---|---|
| at the beginning of June | **all'inizio di giugno**<br>al-lee**neets**-yo dee **joon**-yo |
| at the end of June | **alla fine di giugno**<br>**al**-la **fee**nay dee **joon**-yo |
| before summer | **prima dell'estate**<br>**pree**ma **del**-les-**ta**tay |
| during the summer | **durante l'estate**<br>doo-**ran**tay les-**ta**tay |
| after summer | **dopo l'estate**<br>**do**po les-**ta**tay |

## Time

The 24-hour clock is used a lot more in Italy than in Britain. After 12.00 midday, it continues: 13.00 – **le tredici**; 14.00 – **le quattordici**; 15.00 – **le quindici**, etc. until 24.00 – **le ventiquattro**. With the 24-hour clock, the words **quarto** (quarter) and **mezzo** (half) aren't used:

| | |
|---|---|
| 13.15 | **le tredici e quindici** |
| 13.30 | **le tredici e trenta** |
| 22.45 | **le ventidue e quarantacinque** |

| | |
|---|---|
| What time is it, please? | **Scusi, che ore sono?**<br>**skoo**zee, kay **o**ray **so**no? |
| It's... | **Sono...**<br>**so**no... |

| | |
|---|---|
| 2 o'clock | **le due**<br>lay **doo**ay |
| 3 o'clock | **le tre**<br>lay tray |
| 6 o'clock (etc.) | **le sei**<br>lay say |
| It's 1 o'clock | **È l'una**<br>**e loo**na |
| It's midday | **È mezzogiorno**<br>**e** medz-zo-**jor**no |
| It's midnight | **È mezzanotte**<br>**e** medz-za-**not**-tay |
| 9 | **le nove**<br>lay **no**vay |
| 9.10 | **le nove e dieci**<br>lay **no**vay ay dee-**e**-chee |
| quarter past 9 | **le nove e un quarto**<br>lay **no**vay ay oon **kwar**to |
| 9.20 | **le nove e venti**<br>lay **no**vay ay **ven**tee |
| half past 9 | **le nove e mezza**<br>lay **no**vay ay **medz**-za |
| 9.35 | **le nove e trentacinque**<br>lay **no**vay ay traynta-**cheen**-kway |
| quarter to 10 | **le dieci meno un quarto**<br>lay dee-**e**-chee mayno oon **kwar**to |
| 5 minutes to 10 | **le dieci meno cinque**<br>lay dee-**e**-chee mayno **cheen**-kway |

# Time phrases

| | |
|---|---|
| When does it open/close? | **A che ora apre/chiude?**<br>a kay **o**ra **a**pray/kee-**oo**day? |
| When does it begin/finish? | **A che ora comincia/finisce?**<br>a kay **o**ra ko-**meen**cha/fee-**nee**shay? |
| at 3 o'clock | **alle tre**<br>**al**-lay tray |
| before 3 o'clock | **prima delle tre**<br>**pree**ma **del**-lay tray |
| after 3 o'clock | **dopo le tre**<br>**do**po lay tray |
| today | **oggi**<br>**od**jee |
| tonight | **stasera**<br>sta-**say**ra |
| tomorrow | **domani**<br>do-**ma**nee |
| yesterday | **ieri**<br>**ye**ree |

Reference

# Eating out

## Eating places

**Bar-Caffè** Many bars serve food: generally salads, sandwiches, pasta dishes and pizzas.

**Pizzeria** Pizzas. Take-away food, ***da asporto***, is now popular.

**Pasticceria** Cake shop. These sometimes have a café attached where you can sample the cakes.

**Trattoria** Generally family-run restaurants that offer local food, but tend to have less choice than a **ristorante**.

**Rosticceria** Sells spit-roasted chicken and food to be eaten there (generally standing). Well worth trying.

**Ristorante** The menu and prices are usually displayed outside the entrance. Restaurants are open from about mid-day to 2.30 pm and from 7 pm to 10.30 pm.

**Paninoteca** Sandwich bar.

**Bibite** Soft drinks.

**Toast Farciti** Toasted sandwiches with extra filling such as tomato and gherkin.

**Tavola Calda** Self-service type restaurant which is good for a quick meal.

**Gelateria** Ice-cream bar which also serves drinks.

# In a bar/café

If you just ask for **un caffè** you'll be served **un espresso**, a tiny strong black coffee, so specify the type of coffee you want:

| | |
|---|---|
| **espresso**<br>es**pres**-so | strong small black coffee |
| **cappuccino**<br>kap-poo**chee**no | frothy white coffee |
| **caffè americano**<br>kaf-**fe** ameree**ka**no | black filter coffee |
| **caffè corretto**<br>kaf-**fe** kor-**ret**-to | coffee laced with grappa/brandy |

**FACE TO FACE**

A **Che cosa prende?**
kay **ko**za **pren**-day?
What will you have?

B **Un tè al latte, per favore**
oon **te** al **lat**-tay, payr fa-**vo**ray
A tea with milk, please

| | |
|---|---|
| a coffee | **un caffè**<br>oon kaf-**fe** |
| a lager | **una birra**<br>oona **beer**-ra |
| an orangeade | **un'aranciata**<br>oon aran-**cha**ta |
| with lemon | **col limone**<br>kol lee-**mo**nay |
| no sugar | **senza zucchero**<br>**sen**tsa **tsook**-kayro |

| | |
|---|---|
| for two | **per due**<br>payr **doo**ay |
| for me | **per me**<br>payr me |
| for him/her | **per lui/lei**<br>payr **loo**-ee/lay |
| for us | **per noi**<br>payr noy |
| with ice | **con ghiaccio**<br>kon **gyat**-cho |
| a bottle of mineral water | **una bottiglia d'acqua minerale**<br>oona bot-**teel**-ya **da**kwa meenay-**ra**lay |
| sparkling | **gassata**<br>gas-**sa**ta |
| still | **naturale**<br>natoo-**ra**lay |

## Other drinks to try

**analcolico** non-alcoholic, slightly bitter drink served as apéritif
**chinotto** fizzy soft drink with taste of bitter orange
**cioccolata calda** rich-tasting hot chocolate
**crodino** slightly bitter, non-alcoholic apéritif
**lemonsoda** fizzy drink with taste of real lemons
**spremuta di...** freshly-squeezed juice: ***pompelmo*** – grapefruit

# Reading the menu

If you were planning to eat a full Italian meal, you would begin with **antipasto** (starter), then **primo** (often pasta), then **secondo** (meat or fish), and end with fruit or **dolce** (dessert). This requires some time, so people often skip one or two of the courses.

**Pane - Coperto** Cover charge (**pane** is bread)

**Menù Turistico 7 € 50** Tourist menu often including wine

**Menù a prezzo fisso (solo pranzo)** Set-price menu (lunch only)

**Piatti da asporto** Take-away dishes

| | |
|---|---|
| **Menù** | Menu |
| **Pane Coperto** | Cover charge |
| **Antipasti** | Starters (often cold meats) |
| **Primi Piatti** | First Course (often pasta) |
| **Secondi Piatti** | Main Course (meat or fish) |
| **Contorni** | Vegetables |
| **Formaggi** | Cheese |
| **Frutta** | Fruit |
| **Dolci** | Sweet |

# In a restaurant

**FACE TO FACE**

A **Vorrei prenotare un tavolo per ... persone**
vor-**ray** preno-**ta**ray oon **ta**-volo payr ... per-**so**nay
I'd like to book a table for ... people

B **Sì, per quando?**
see, payr **kwan**do?
Yes, when for?

A **Per questa sera.../per domani sera.../alle otto**
payr **kwes**ta **say**ra.../payr do-**ma**nee **say**ra.../ **al**-lay **ot**-to
For tonight.../for tomorrow night.../at 8 o'clock

| | |
|---|---|
| The menu, please | **Il menù per favore**<br>eel me**noo** payr fa-**vo**ray |
| What is the dish of the day? | **Qual è il piatto del giorno?**<br>kwal **e** eel **pyat**-to del **jor**no? |
| Do you have a tourist menu? | **Avete il menù turistico?**<br>a-**vay**tay eel me**noo** too-**rees**teeko? |
| at a set price? | **a prezzo fisso?**<br>a **prets**-so **fees**-so? |
| What is the speciality of the house? | **Qual è la specialità della casa?**<br>kwal **e** la spetchalee-**ta del**-la **ka**za? |

| | |
|---|---|
| Can you tell me what this is? | **Mi può spiegare che cos'è questo?**<br>mee pw**o** spyay-**ga**ray kay ko-**ze** **kwes**to? |
| I'll have this | **Prendo questo**<br>**pren**do **kwes**to |
| Could we have some more bread/more water, please? | **Ci dà ancora un po' di pane/ un po' di acqua per favore?**<br>chee **da** an-**ko**ra oon po dee **pa**nay/ oon po dee **a**kwa payr fa-**vo**ray? |
| The bill, please | **Il conto per favore**<br>eel **kon**to payr fa-**vo**ray |
| Is service included? | **Il servizio è incluso?**<br>eel ser**veets**-yo e een-**kloo**so? |

## Vegetarian

Don't expect great things – Italians love good meat.

| | |
|---|---|
| Are there any vegetarian restaurants here? | **Ci sono dei ristoranti per vegetariani?**<br>chee **so**no day reesto-**ran**tee payr ved-jay-tar-**ya**nee? |
| Do you have any vegetarian dishes? | **Avete dei piatti per vegetariani?**<br>a-**vay**tay day **pyat**-tee payr ved-jay-tar-**ya**nee? |

| | |
|---|---|
| Which dishes have no meat/fish? | **Quali piatti non hanno carne/ pesce?**<br>**kwa**lee **pyat**-tee non **an**-no **kar**-nay/**pay**shay? |
| What fish dishes do you have? | **Quali piatti di pesce avete?**<br>**kwa**lee **pyat**-tee dee **pay**shay a-**vay**tay? |
| I'd like pasta as a main course | **Vorrei un piatto di pasta come secondo**<br>vor-**ray** oon **pyat**-to dee **pas**ta **ko**may se**kon**do |
| I don't like meat | **Non mi piace la carne**<br>non mee pee-**a**-chay la **kar**-nay |
| What do you recommend? | **Che cosa mi consiglia?**<br>kay **ko**za mee kon-**see**lya? |
| Is it made with vegetable stock? | **È fatto con dadi vegetariani?**<br>**e fat**-to kon **da**dee ved-jay-tar-**ya**nee? |

## Possible dishes

**insalata mista** mixed salad (lettuce, tomato, peppers, etc.)
**insalata tricolore** mozzarella, tomato and fresh basil
**minestrone** thick vegetable soup
**pasta al pomodoro** pasta with tomato sauce
**pasta al pesto** pasta with basil, garlic and pinenut sauce

**peperonata** sweet pepper and tomato stew

**pizza (*margherita*, *ai funghi*, *vegetariana*)** various pizzas

**polenta uncia** maize porridge with butter, garlic and cheese

**riso in bianco** boiled rice with butter, garlic, black pepper

# Wines and spirits

| | |
|---|---|
| The wine list, please | **La lista dei vini per favore**<br>la **lees**ta day **vee**nee payr fa-**vo**ray |
| white wine | **vino bianco**<br>**vee**no **byan**-ko |
| red wine | **vino rosso**<br>**vee**no **ros**-so |
| Can you recommend a good local wine? | **Ci può consigliare un buon vino locale?**<br>chee pu**o** konseel-**ya**ray oon bwon **vee**no lo-**ka**lay? |
| A bottle... | **Una bottiglia...**<br>oona bot-**teel**-ya... |
| A carafe... | **Una caraffa...**<br>oona ka-**raf**-fa... |
| of house wine | **di vino della casa**<br>dee **vee**no **del**-la **ka**za |

Wines and spirits

## Wines

**Asti Spumante** sparkling sweet or semi-sweet white wine often drunk for celebrations. Produced in the Asti district of Piedmont

**Barbaresco** dry, full-bodied red wine from Piedmont

**Barbera** dry, spicy red wine from Piedmont

**Bardolino** light, dry red or rosé wine from the Veneto

**Barolo** good, full-bodied red wine from Piedmont

**Brunello di Montalcino** superior, powerful red wine from Tuscany

**Chianti** full, fruity red wine from Tuscany

**Chiaretto** light, rosé-style wine from the Veneto

**Cinqueterre** dry, light and fragrant white wines from Liguria

**Est! Est! Est!** crisp, fruity white wine from region near Rome

**Frascati** crisp, fresh, dry to off-dry white wine from near Rome

**Lacrima christi** full-bodied wine from Campania and Sicily

**Lambrusco** slightly sparkling wine from Emilia-Romagna

**Marsala** dark dessert wine from Sicily

**Merlot** good, dry red wine from NE Italy

**Montepulciano** dry or sweet red wine from Tuscany

**Moscato** sweet, aromatic white wine from NW Italy
**Nebbiolo** light, red wine from Piedmont
**Orvieto** crisp, smooth, dry white wine from Umbria
**Pinot bianco** dry white wine from NE Italy
**Savuto** dry red wine from Calabria
**Soave** dry white wine from the Veneto
**Valpolicella** light, fruity red wine from the Veneto
**Verdicchio** fresh, dry white wine from the Marches
**Verduzzo** dry, tangy white wine from NE Italy
**Vernaccia di San Gimignano** dry white wine from Tuscany
**Vino da tavola** table wine
**Vino della casa** house wine
**Vin Santo** golden, scented wine ranging from sweet to dry

## Spirits and liqueurs

| | |
|---|---|
| What liqueurs do you have? | **Quali liquori avete?** **kwa**lee lee-**kwo**ree a-**vay**tay? |

**Amaretto** strong, sweet almond-flavoured liqueur
**Cynar** strongly flavoured artichoke-based digestivo
**Digestivo** slightly bitter, herb-flavoured liqueur to help digestion
**Grappa** strong spirit from grape pressings, often added to coffee
**Sambuca** aniseed liqueur, served with coffee beans and set alight
**Strega** stong herb-flavoured liqueur
**Vecchia Romagna** Italian brandy

# Menu reader

**abbacchio** suckling or milk-fed lamb, usually eaten at Easter. Roasted with garlic and rosemary
**acciughe** anchovies
**acciughe ripiene** stuffed fresh anchovies
**aceto** vinegar
**aceto balsamico** balsamic vinegar
**acqua brillante** tonic water
**acqua cotta** traditional Tuscan soup made from onions, peppers, celery and tomato. Beaten eggs and parmesan are added just before serving
**acqua minerale** mineral water; this can be still (**naturale**), with gas (**effervescente naturale**), or with added gas (**gassata/frizzante**)
**affettato misto** selection of cold meats
**affogato** poached
**affogato al caffè** vanilla ice cream with hot espresso coffee poured over it
**affumicato** smoked
**aglio** garlic
**aglio, olio e peperoncino** garlic, olive oil and hot chilli served on pasta
**agnello** lamb
**agnello al forno/arrosto** roast lamb

**agnolotti** pasta squares filled with white meat and cheese, usually served with bolognese sauce
**agro, all'agro** dressing/seasoning for vegetables made with lemon juice or vinegar
**agrodolce** sweet and sour sauce
**ai ferri** grilled
**al, alla** etc means with, or in the style of: e.g. **pasta al sugo** is pasta with tomato sauce, and **pollo alla cacciatora** is chicken hunter-style
**albicocche ripiene** stuffed apricots
**alici** fresh anchovies
**alloro** bayleaf
**amarene** sour cherries
**amaretti** macaroons
**amaro** bitter liqueur drunk to aid digestion
**amatriciana, ...all'** bacon, tomato and onion sauce
**ananas** pineapple
**anatra** duck
**anguilla** eel
**anguille alla Comacchio** stewed eels with tomato and vinegar
**anguille carpionate** fried eels in a vinegar sauce
**anguille in umido** stewed eels
**anguria** watermelon
**anice** aniseed
**antipasto** starter/appetizer
**antipasto misto** selection of cold starters such as ham, salami and pickles

**aperitivo** aperitif
**aragosta** lobster
**arance** oranges
**aranciata** orangeade
**arancini di riso** rice croquettes filled with minced veal and peas
**arrabbiata, ...all'** tomato sauce with bacon, onion, tomatoes and hot chillies
**arrosto** roast meat
**arrosto di maiale/manzo/vitello** roast pork/beef/veal
**asparagi** asparagus
**astice** crayfish

**baccalà** salted cod
**baccalà alla fiorentina** salted cod cooked in tomato sauce
**baccalà alla vicentina** salted cod cooked in milk with anchovies, garlic and parsley
**baccalà alla livornese** salted cod cooked in a tomato sauce
**bagna cauda** hot garlic and anchovy dip
**banana** banana
**basilico** basil
**Bel Paese** soft mild cheese
**ben cotto** well done
**besciamella** béchamel sauce
**bianco ...in** white, pasta or rice served with butter or olive oil and parmesan cheese

**bietola** beetroot
**birra** lager-type beer; draught beer is **birra alla spina**
**biscotti** biscuits
**bistecca** steak
**bistecca fiorentina** thickly cut, charcoal-grilled T-bone steak
**bistecchini di cinghiale** wild boar steaks
**bitter** non-alcoholic, bitter drink served as an aperitif
**bocconcini di vitello** pieces of veal cooked in wine and butter
**bollito** boiled
**bollito misto** different kinds of meat and vegetables boiled together
**bolognese, ...alla** tomato and minced meat sauce, served with parmesan
**bonet alla Piemontese** chocolate pudding made with biscuits, macaroons and rum
**borlotti** dried red haricot beans
**boscaiola, ...alla** with mushroom and ham sauce
**brace, ...alla** grilled
**braciola** rib steak/chop
**brasato** beef stew
**bresaola** dried cured beef
**brodetto di pesce** fish soup
**brodo** bouillon or broth
**bucatini** thick spaghetti-like pasta with a hole running through it

**budino** a blancmange-type pudding
**burro** butter
**burro, ...al** fried in butter
**burro e salvia** butter and sage sauce
**busecca** rich tripe and cheese soup

**cacciatora, ...alla** meat or game, hunter-style – cooked with tomato, herbs, garlic and wine
**cachi** persimmons
**caciocavallo** cow's cheese, quite strong when mature
**caffè** coffee – if you ask for **un caffè** you'll be served **un espresso** (small, strong and black)
**caffè americano** black filter coffee
**caffè corretto** coffee laced with spirit
**caffè doppio** a large coffee (twice normal size)
**caffelatte** milky coffee
**calamaretti imbottiti** baby squid stuffed with breadcrumbs and anchovies
**calamari** squid
**calamari fritti** battered fried squid rings
**calzone** folded over pizza with filling
**camomilla** camomile tea
**canederli tirolesi** Tyrolean dumplings made with smoked cured ham and bread
**cannella** cinnamon
**cannellini** small white beans
**cannelloni** meat-filled pasta tubes covered with béchamel sauce and baked. Vegetarian options are filled with spinach and ricotta

**cannoli** fried pastries stuffed with ricotta, candied fruit and bitter chocolate
**cantucci** nutty biscuits
**caponata** Sicilian dish of aubergines, potatoes and peppers, cooked in a sweet and sour sauce
**cappelletti** literally 'little hats' filled with cheese or meat filling, served with bolognese meat sauce or in broth
**capperi** capers
**cappon magro** an elaborate salad of cold seafood, fish and cooked vegetables
**cappuccino** frothy white coffee
**caprese** tomato and mozzarella salad with basil
**capretto** baby goat (kid)
**caprino** soft goat's cheese
**caramelle** sweets
**carbonara, ...alla** with a smoked bacon, egg, cream and parmesan sauce
**carciofi** artichokes
**carciofi alla Giudia** young artichokes, flattened and deep-fried
**carciofi alla romana, carciofi ripieni** artichokes stuffed with breadcrumbs, parsley and anchovies
**cardi** cardoons (similar to fennel)
**carne** meat
**carote** carrots
**carpaccio** raw sliced lean beef eaten with lemon juice, olive oil and thickly grated parmesan cheese
**carpa** carp

**carpione, in** pickled in vinegar, wine and lemon juice
**casalinga, ...alla** home-made style
**cassata** layers of ice cream with candied fruits
**cassata alla siciliana** sponge dessert with ricotta and candied fruits
**castagnaccio** chestnut cake
**castagne** chestnuts
**cavolfiore** cauliflower
**cavolo** cabbage
**ceci** chickpeas
**cefalo** grey mullet
**cena** dinner
**cervella** calves' brains, usually fried
**cetriolo** cucumber
**ciambella** ring-shaped fruit cake
**ciambellini** ring-shaped aniseed biscuits
**cicoria** chicory
**ciliegie** cherries
**cime di rapa** leafy, green vegetable similar to turnip tops, often served with orecchiette
**cinghiale** wild boar
**cioccolata calda** rich hot chocolate drink, often served with whipped cream
**cioccolatini** chocolates
**cioccolato** chocolate
**cipolle** onions
**cocco** coconut
**cocomero** watermelon
**coda di bue** oxtail

**colomba** bird-shaped cake with orange peel, topped with sugared almonds, eaten at Easter
**conchiglie** shell-shaped pasta
**confetti** sugared almonds
**coniglio** rabbit
  **coniglio in umido** rabbit stew
**contorni** vegetable side dishes
**cornetto** ice-cream cone; a croissant filled with jam, custard or chocolate
**cosciotto d'agnello all'abruzzese** braised leg of lamb with garlic, tomatoes, rosemary and wine
**cotechino** spicy pork sausage boiled and served with lentils
**cotoletta** cutlet/chop
  **cotoletta al prosciutto** veal cutlet with a slice of Parma ham
  **cotoletta alla bolognese** veal cutlet topped with ham and cheese
  **cotoletta alla milanese** veal cutlet dipped in egg and breadcrumbs then fried
  **cotoletta alla valdostana** breaded veal chop topped with Fontina cheese and ham
**cotto** cooked
**cozze** mussels
**crema di...** cream soup or sauce/custard
**crêpe** pancake
**crespella** stuffed pancake
**crocchette di patate** potato croquettes
**crostata** tart, usually filled with jam

**crostata di frutta** tart filled with fruit and glazed
**crostini** croutons
**crostini di fegatini** chicken liver pâté on toast
**crudo** raw
**cuori di carciofo** artichoke hearts
**dente, ...al** pasta cooked so it is still quite firm
**dentice** sea bream
**dolce** dessert
**dolcelatte** soft, creamy blue cheese
**dragoncello** tarragon

**entrecote** steak

**fagiano** pheasant
**fagiano con funghi** pheasant with porcini mushrooms
**fagiano in salmì** pheasant stewed in wine
**fagioli** beans
**fagioli al tonno** haricot beans with tuna fish in olive oil
**fagioli con cotiche** bean stew with pork rinds
**fagiolini** green beans
**faraona** guinea fowl
**farcito** stuffed
**farfalle** butterfly-shaped pasta
**fave** broad beans
**fave al guanciale** broad beans cooked with bacon and onion
**fegatini di pollo** chicken livers

**fegato** liver (mainly calves')
**fegato alla veneziana** calves' liver fried in butter and onion
**ferri, ...ai** grilled without oil
**fettuccine** fresh ribbon pasta
**fichi** figs
**fichi d'India** prickly pears
**filetto** fillet steak
**filetto di tacchino alla bolognese** turkey breast served with a slice of ham and cheese
**finanziera, ...alla** mince of chicken livers, mushrooms and wine sauce
**finocchio** fennel
**fiori di zucchini** courgette flowers
**focaccia** flat bread brushed with salt and olive oil, sprinkled with herbs or onions
**fonduta** cheese fondue
**Fontina** mild to strong cow's milk cheese
**formaggio** cheese
**forno, ...al** baked
**fragole** strawberries
**frittata** omlette
**fritto** fried
**fritto misto** selection of fried seafood
**frullato di frutta** fruit smoothie
**frutta** fruit
**frutti di bosco** fruits of the forest
**frutti di mare** shellfish/seafood
**funghi** mushrooms

**funghi trifolati** sliced mushrooms fried with garlic and parsley
**fusilli** spiral-shaped pasta

**gamberi** prawns
**gamberoni** giant prawns
**gazzosa** fizzy bottled lemonade
**gelato** ice cream
**gelato misto** a selection of ice creams
**girasole** sunflower
**gnocchi** small dumplings made from potato and flour. Boiled and served with tomato sauce or ragù
**gnocchi alla romana** dumplings made from semolina, butter and parmesan, oven-baked
**gnocchi verdi** spinach and potato dumplings
**gorgonzola** a strong blue cows' milk cheese
**granchio** crab
**grana** hard cows'milk cheese; generic name given to Parmesan cheese
**granita** slush puppy, crushed ice drink
**granita al caffè** cold coffee with crushed ice
**grappa** strong spirit from grape pressings
**grattugiato** grated
**griglia, ...alla** grilled
**grigliata mista** mixed grill
**grissini** breadsticks
**guanciale** streaky bacon made from pig's cheek
**insalata** salad
**insalata caprese** tomato, basil and mozzarella salad

**insalata di mare** mixed seafood salad
**insalata di pomodori** tomato salad
**insalata di riso** rice salad
**insalata mista** mixed salad
**insalata russa** cold diced vegetables served with mayonnaise
**insalata verde** green salad
**involtini** rolls of veal or pork stuffed in various ways

**lamponi** raspberries
**latte** milk
**lattuga** lettuce
**lenticchie** lentils
**lepre** hare
**lepre in salmì** hare stewed in wine
**lesso** boiled
**limone** lemon
**limoncello** lemon liqueur
**lingua** tongue
**linguine** flat spaghetti
**lombata di maiale** pork chop
**lonza** type of pork fillet
**luccio** pike
**lumache** snails

**maccheroni** macaroni
**maccheroni ai quattro formaggi** pasta with four cheeses
**macedonia** fresh fruit salad

**macinata** mince
**magro, di** a meatless dish (often a fish alternative)
**maiale** pork
**maionese** mayonnaise
**mandorle** almonds
**manzo** beef
**marmellata** jam
**marsala** dark dessert wine from Sicily
**mascarpone** rich cream cheese
**mela** apple
**melagrana** pomegranate
**melanzane** aubergines
**melanzane alla Parmigiana** layers of fried aubergine baked with tomato sauce, ham, parmesan and mozzarella
**melanzane ripiene** stuffed aubergines
**melone** melon
**menta** mint
**meringata** meringue and ice cream dessert
**merluzzo** cod
**miele** honey
**milanese, ...alla** normally applied to veal cutlets dipped in egg and breadcrumbs before frying
**minestra** soup
**minestrone** vegetable soup (with either pasta or rice)
**mirtilli** blueberries
**misto di funghi** mixed mushrooms
**more** blackberries
**mortadella** type of salami

**mostarda** pickled fruit. Served with **bollito** (boiled meats)
**mozzarella** fresh cheese preserved in whey, used in pizzas
**mozzarella di bufala** mozzarella made with buffalo milk
**mozzarella in carrozza** mozzarella sandwiched in bread, dipped in egg and breadcrumbs and fried
**mugnaia, ...alla** usually fish dusted in flour then fried in butter

**napoletana, ...alla** with tomato-based sauce
**nocciole** hazelnuts
**noci** walnuts
**norma, ...alla** tomato and fried aubergine sauce
**olio** oil
**olio d'oliva** olive oil
**olive** olives
**orecchiette** ear-shaped pasta, served with either tomato sauce or **cime di rapa** (type of broccoli)
**origano** oregano
**orzata** cool, milky drink made from barley
**ossobuco** marrow-bone veal steak
**ostriche** oysters

**paglia e fieno** green and plain ribbon pasta
**pan pepato** sweet loaf with mixed nuts and spices
**pancetta** streaky bacon
**pandoro** soft cork-shaped yeast cake

**pane** bread
**pane e coperto** cover charge
**pane integrale** wholemeal bread
**panettone** cork-shaped yeast cake with orange peel and raisins
**panforte** a hard, dried-fruit and nut cake
**panino** bread roll or sandwich
**panna** cream
**pansotti** pasta squares filled with herbs and cheese
**panzerotti** folded pizza dough stuffed with mozzarella, salami and ham, usually fried
**pappardelle** wide ribbon-shaped pasta
**pappardelle al sugo di lepre** wide ribbon pasta with hare, wine and tomato sauce
**parmigiana di melanzane** aubergine layers, oven-baked with tomato sauce and parmesan cheese
**parmigiano** parmesan cheese
**pasta al forno** pasta baked with minced meat, eggs, tomato and cheese
**pasta all'uovo** fresh pasta made with eggs
**pasta asciutta** pasta served with a sauce, such as **spaghetti al sugo**, and not in a soup form, such as **ravioli in brodo** (ravioli in bouillon)
**pasta e fagioli** pasta with beans
**pasta fresca** fresh pasta
**pasticcio** pie
**pastina in brodo** pasta pieces in clear broth
**patate** potatoes
**patate fritte** chips

**patatine** crisps
**patatine fritte** french fries
**pecorino** hard tangy sheep's milk cheese
**penne** quill-shaped pasta
**pepe** pepper
**peperonata** ratatouille
**peperoncino** hot chilli pepper
**peperoni** peppers
**peperoni ripieni** stuffed peppers
**pere** pears
**pesca** peach
**pescanoce** nectarine
**pesce** fish
**pesce arrosto** baked fish
**pesce persico** perch
**pesce spada** swordfish
**pesto** sauce of pounded basil, garlic, pine-nuts, olive oil and Parmesan cheese
**petto di pollo** chicken breast
**piatto** dish
**piatto del giorno** dish of the day
**piatti tipici** regional dishes
**pietanze** main courses
**pinoli** pine nuts
**pinzoccheri** buckwheat pasta noodles
**piselli** peas
**pistacchio** pistachio
**pizza** originally from Naples, cooked in wood-burning ovens

**pizza ai funghi** mushroom pizza
**pizza alla Siciliana** pizza with tomato, anchovy, black olives and capers
**pizza capricciosa** pizza with baby artichoke, ham and egg
**pizza ai frutti di mare** pizza with seafood
**pizza margherita** named after the first queen of a united Italy, symbolising the colours of the Italian flag: red (tomatoes), green (basil) and white (mozzarella)
**pizza marinara** tomato and garlic pizza
**pizza Napoli/Napoletana** pizza with tomato, cheese, anchovy, olive oil and oregano
**pizza quattro formaggi** a pizza divided into four sections, each with a different cheese topping
**pizza quattro stagioni** pizza divided into four sections with a selection of toppings on each

**pizzaiola, ...alla** cooked with tomatoes, garlic and herbs
**pizzetta** small cheese and tomato pizza
**polenta** coarse corn or maize porridge
**polenta uncia** polenta baked with butter, garlic and cheese
**pollame** poultry/fowl
**pollo** chicken
**pollo alla diavola** chicken grilled with herbs and chilli pepper
**pollo alla romana** chicken with tomatoes and peppers

**pollo arrosto** roast chicken
**polpette** beef meatballs made with parmesan and parsley
**polipo** octopus
**polipo affogato** octopus cooked in tomato sauce
**pomodoro** tomato
**pomodoro, ...al** tomato sauce (same as **sugo**)
**pomodori ripieni** stuffed tomatoes
**pompelmo** grapefruit
**porchetta** roast suckling pig
**porcini** prized cep mushrooms, often dried
**porri** leeks
**pranzo** lunch
**prezzemolo** parsley
**prima colazione** breakfast
**primo** first course
**prosciutto** ham
**prosciutto cotto** boiled ham
**prosciutto crudo** cured Parma ham
**prosciutto di cinghiale** cured ham made from wild boar
**prosciutto e melone** Parma ham and melon slices
**prosecco** sparkling dry white wine
**provolone** cow's milk cheese
**prugne** plums
**puttanesca, ...alla** with tomato, garlic, hot chilli, anchovies and capers

**quaglie** quails

**radicchio** red-leaf lettuce
**ragù, ...al** minced meat, tomato and garlic (same as bolognese)
**rana pescatrice** monkfish
**rane** frogs (only the legs are eaten)
**ravioli** pasta cushions filled with meat or cheese and spinach
**ribes** black/redcurrants
**riccio di mare** sea urchin
**ricotta** soft white cheese
**rigatoni** ribbed tubes of pasta
**ripieno** stuffed
**risi e bisi** thick rice and pea soup
**riso** rice
**risotto** rice cooked in broth
  **risotto ai funghi** risotto with porcini mushrooms
  **risotto al nero di seppia** risotto made with squid and its ink
  **risotto alla milanese** risotto flavoured with saffron, parmesan and butter, and cooked in meat broth
  **risotto alla pescatora** seafood rice
**robiola** creamy cheese with a mild taste
**rognone** kidney
**rosmarino** rosemary
**rucola** rocket (in Rome: **rughetta**)

**salame** salami (there are many types)
**sale** salt

**salmone** salmon

**salsa** sauce

**salsa verde** sauce made of olive oil, anchovies, hard boiled egg and parsley

**salsicce** sausages

**saltimbocca alla romana** veal cooked in white wine with Parma ham

**salvia** sage

**sampietro** John Dory (type of fish)

**sangue, ...al** rare

**sarde** sardines

**sarde al beccafico** sardines marinated and stuffed with breadcrumbs, pecorino cheese, garlic and parsley, then fried

**sarde in saor** fried sardines marinated in vinegar, onions, sultanas and pine nuts

**sartù di riso** rice and meat timbale (rather like a pie)

**scaloppine** veal escalopes

**scaloppine alla milanese** veal escalopes dipped in egg, breadcrumbs and fried in butter

**scaloppine alla pizzaiola** thinly sliced steak fried in a tomato and herb sauce

**scamorza** a soft cow's milk cheese (type of dried mozzarella)

**scamorza affumicata** smoked scamorza

**scampi** scampi

**secondo** second course, usually meat or fish

**sedano** celery

**selz** soda water

**semifreddo** chilled dessert made with ice cream
**senape** mustard
**seppia** cuttlefish
**servizio compreso** service included
**sfogliatelle** puff pastry cakes
**sgombro** mackerel
**soffritto** sliced onion and/or garlic fried in olive oil
**sogliola** sole
**sott'olio** in olive oil
**spaghetti** spaghetti
**spaghetti alla chitarra** square-shaped pasta
**spaghetti all'amatriciana** spaghetti with bacon, onion and tomato sauce
**speck** type of smoked, cured ham
**spezzatino** stew
**spiedini** meat kebabs
**spiedo, ...allo** spit-roasted, or on a skewer
**spinaci** spinach
**spremuta** freshly squeezed fruit juice
**spremuta di pompelmo** fresh grapefruit juice
**spumante** sparkling wine
**stoccafisso** dried stockfish
**stracciatella** consommé with egg stirred in and grated parmesan; or ice-cream with chocolate chips
**stracotto** braised beef slow-cooked with vegetables
**succo di frutta** bottled fruit juice
**sugo** sauce, often refers to the basic tomato, basil and garlic sauce (same as **al pomodoro**)
**surgelato** frozen

**tacchino** turkey
**tagliata** thinly-sliced meat, briefly cooked on a griddle and served with herbs or parmesan chips
**tagliata di pesce spada** thinly-sliced swordfish
**tagliatelle** ribbon-like pasta often served in cream sauce
**taleggio** soft, creamy cheese similar to camembert
**tartine** canapés
**tartufi** truffles: black (**nero**) and white (**bianco**) are used extensively in risotto and game dishes
  **tartufo di cioccolato** rich chocolate ice cream shaped like a truffle
**tè** tea. Normally served with lemon (**al limone**). If you want it with milk you must ask for **tè al latte**
**timballo** a baked pie
**timo** thyme
**tinca** tench
**tiramisù** dessert made with mascarpone, sponge, coffee and marsala
**tonica** tonic water
**tonno** tuna fish
  **tonno, ...al** tuna sauce
  **tonno e fagioli** tuna and bean salad
**torrone** nougat
**torta** cake/flan/tart
**tortellini** meat-filled pasta cushions
  **tortellini panna e prosciutto** tortellini served with cream and ham
**tramezzini** sliced white bread with mixed fillings

**trenette** long thin strips of pasta
**triglia** red mullet
**triglia alla livornese** red mullet fried with chillies in tomato sauce
**trippa** tripe, often cooked with tomatoes and onions
**trota** trout

**umido ... in** stewed
**uova** eggs
**uova alla fiorentina** poached eggs on spinach tarts
**uva** grapes
**uva passa** raisins

**vaniglia** vanilla
**verdure** vegetables
**vermicelli** very thin pasta
**vermut** vermouth
**verza** Savoy (green) cabbage
**vino** wine
**vin brûlé** mulled wine
**vino bianco** white wine
**vino dolce** sweet wine
**vino frizzante** sparkling wine
**vino rosato** rosé wine
**vino rosso** red wine
**vino secco** dry wine
**vitello** veal
**vongole** clams
**vongole, ...alle** with clams, parsley, garlic and olive oil

**wurstel** Frankfurter sausages

**zabaglione** frothy dessert made with egg yolks and sugar beaten with marsala over heat
**zafferano** saffron, used in risotto alla milanese
**zampone** pig's trotter filled with spicy sausage
**zola** soft cheese similar to gorgonzola but sweeter
**zucca** marrow, pumpkin
**zucchero** sugar
**zucchini** courgettes
**zuccotto** rich cream, coffee and nut pudding
**zuppa** soup
**zuppa di cozze** mussel soup
**zuppa di fagioli** bean soup
**zuppa inglese** dessert similar to trifle laced with whisky or vermouth
**zuppa pavese** a bread soup with broth and poached eggs, topped with grated cheese

# Nouns

A noun is a word such as *car*, *horse* or *Mary*, which is used to refer to a person or thing. In Italian all nouns are either masculine or feminine. Their gender is shown in the article (**il**, **la**, **un**, **una**, etc.).



| | masculine singular | feminine singular |
|---|---|---|
| the | **il**<br>**l'** (+vowel)<br>**lo** (+z, gn, pn, ps, x, s+consonant) | **la**<br>**l'** (+vowel) |
| | **masculine plural** | **feminine plural** |
| | **i**<br>**gli** (+vowel, +z, gn, pn, s+consonant) | **le** |

| | masculine | feminine |
|---|---|---|
| a, an | **un**<br>**uno** (+z, gn, pn, s+consonant) | **una**<br>**un'** (+vowel) |

# Formation of plurals

For most nouns, the singular ending changes as follows:

| masc. singular | masc. plural | example |
|---|---|---|
| o | i | **libro** → **libri** |
| e | i | **padre** → **padri** |
| a | i | **artista** → **artisti** |

NOTE: Most nouns ending in **co** and **go** become **chi** and **ghi** in the plural to keep the **c** and **g** hard sounding. Some exceptions occur in the masculine, e.g. **amico** → **amici**.

| fem. singular | fem. plural | example |
|---|---|---|
| a | e | **mela** → **mele** |
| e | i | **madre** → **madri** |

NOTE: Nouns ending in **ca** and **ga** become **che** and **ghe** in the plural to keep the **c** and **g** hard sounding. Nouns ending in **cia** and **gia** often become **ce** and **ge** to keep the **c** and **g** soft sounding, e.g.:

**la barca** → **le barche**
**la boccia** → **le bocce**

# Adjectives

An adjective is a word such as *small*, *pretty* or *practical* that describes a person or thing, or gives extra information about them.

Adjectives normally follow the noun they describe in Italian, e.g. **la mela** <u>**rossa**</u> (the <u>red</u> apple).

Some common exceptions which tend to go before the noun are:

**bello** beautiful, **breve** short, **brutto** ugly, **buono** good, **cattivo** bad, **giovane** young, **grande** big, **lungo** long, **nuovo** new, **piccolo** small, **vecchio** old

e.g. **una** <u>**bella**</u> **giornata** (a <u>beautiful</u> day).

Italian adjectives have to reflect the gender of the noun they describe. To make an adjective *feminine*, an **a** replaces the **o** of the *masculine*, e.g. **rosso** – **rossa**. Adjectives ending in **e**, e.g. **giovane**, can be either *masculine* or *feminine*. The plural forms of the adjective change in the way described for nouns (above).

Grammar

Grammar

# My, your, his, her, our, their

These words also depend on the gender and number of the noun they accompany, and not on the sex of the 'owner'.

| | with masc. sing. noun | with fem. sing. noun | with masc. plur. noun | with fem. plur. noun |
|---|---|---|---|---|
| **my** | **il mio** | **la mia** | **i miei** | **le mie** |
| **your** *(polite)* | **il suo** | **la sua** | **i suoi** | **le sue** |
| **your** *(familiar)* | **il tuo** | **la tua** | **i tuoi** | **le tue** |
| **your** *(plural)* | **il vostro** | **la vostra** | **i vostri** | **le vostre** |
| **his/her** | **il suo** | **la sua** | **i suoi** | **le sue** |
| **our** | **il nostro** | **la nostra** | **i nostri** | **le nostre** |
| **their** | **il loro** | **la loro** | **i loro** | **le loro** |

# Pronouns

A pronoun is a word that you use to refer to someone or something when you do not need to use a noun, often because the person or thing has been mentioned earlier. Examples are *it*, *she*, *something* and *myself*.

| subject | | object | |
|---|---|---|---|
| **I** | **io** | **me** | **mi** |
| **you** | **lei** | **you** | **la** |
| **he** | **lui/egli** | **him** | **lo/l'** (+vowel) |
| **she** | **lei/ella** | **her** | **la/l'** (+vowel) |
| **it** (*masc.*) | **esso** | **it** (*masc.*) | **lo/l'** (+vowel) |
| **it** (*fem.*) | **essa** | **it** (*fem.*) | **la/l'** (+vowel) |
| **we** | **noi** | **us** | **ci** |
| **you** | **voi** | **you** | **vi** |
| **they** | **loro** | **them** (*masc.*) | **li** |
| (things *masc.*) | **essi** | **them** (*fem.*) | **le** |
| (things *fem.*) | **esse** | | |

Subject pronouns (**io**, **tu**, **egli**, etc.) are often omitted in Italian, since the verb ending generally distinguishes the person:

**parlo** → I speak
**parliamo** → we speak

In Italian there are two forms for *you* – **Lei** (*singular*) and **voi** (*plural*). **Tu**, the familiar form for *you*, should only be used with people you know well, or children.

The object pronouns shown above are also used to mean *to me*, *to us*, etc., except:

**to him/to it** → **gli**
**to her/to it/to you** → **le**
**to them** → **loro**

Grammar

Object pronouns (other than **loro**) usually go before the verb:

| | | |
|---|---|---|
| **lo vedo** | *but* | **scriverò loro** |
| I see him | | I will write to them |

When used with an infinitive (the verb form given in the dictionary), the pronoun follows and is attached to the infinitive less its final **e**:

**voglio comprarlo** → I want to buy it

# Verbs

A verb is a word such as *sing*, *walk* or *cry*, which is used with a subject to say what someone or something does or what happens to them. Regular verbs follow the same pattern of endings. Irregular verbs do not follow a regular pattern so you need to learn the different endings.

There are three main patterns of endings for verbs in Italian – those ending **-are**, **-ere** and **-ire** in the dictionary. Two examples of the **-ire** verbs are shown, since two distinct groups of endings exist. Subject pronouns are shown in brackets because these are often not used:

| | parlare | to speak |
|---|---|---|
| (io) | **parlo** | I speak |
| (tu) | **parli** | you speak |
| (lui/lei) | **parla** | (s)he speaks |
| (noi) | **parliamo** | we speak |
| (voi) | **parlate** | you speak |
| (loro) | **parlano** | they speak |

*past participle:* **parlato** (with **avere**)

| | vendere | to sell |
|---|---|---|
| (io) | **vendo** | I sell |
| (tu) | **vendi** | you sell |
| (lui/lei) | **vende** | (s)he sells |
| (noi) | **vendiamo** | we sell |
| (voi) | **vendete** | you sell |
| (loro) | **vendono** | they sell |

*past participle:* **venduto** (with **avere**)

| | dormire | to sleep |
|---|---|---|
| (io) | **dormo** | I sleep |
| (tu) | **dormi** | you sleep |
| (lui/lei) | **dorme** | (s)he sleeps |
| (noi) | **dormiamo** | we sleep |
| (voi) | **dormite** | you sleep |
| (loro) | **dormono** | they sleep |

*past participle:* **dormito** (with **avere**)

| | **finire** | **to finish** |
|---|---|---|
| (io) | **finisco** | I finish |
| (tu) | **finisci** | you finish |
| (lui/lei) | **finisce** | (s)he finishes |
| (noi) | **finiamo** | we finish |
| (voi) | **finite** | you finish |
| (loro) | **finiscono** | they finish |

*past participle:* **finito** (with **avere**)

# Irregular verbs

Some important irregular verbs are:

| | **essere** | **to be** | **avere** | **to have** |
|---|---|---|---|---|
| (io) | **sono** | I am | **ho** | I have |
| (tu) | **sei** | you are | **hai** | you have |
| (lui/lei) | **è** | (s)he is | **ha** | (s)he has |
| (noi) | **siamo** | we are | **abbiamo** | we have |
| (voi) | **siete** | you are | **avete** | you have |
| (loro) | **sono** | they are | **hanno** | they have |
| | *past participle:* **stato** (with **essere**) | | *past participle:* **avuto** (with **avere**) | |

| | **andare** | **to go** | **fare** | **to do** |
|---|---|---|---|---|
| (io) | **vado** | I go | **faccio** | I do |
| (tu) | **vai** | you go | **fai** | you do |
| (lui/lei) | **va** | (s)he goes | **fa** | (s)he does |

| | | | | |
|---|---|---|---|---|
| (noi) | **andiamo** | we go | **facciamo** | we do |
| (voi) | **andate** | you go | **fate** | you do |
| (loro) | **vanno** | they go | **fanno** | they do |
| | *past participle:* | | *past participle:* | |
| | **andato** (with **essere**) | | **fatto** (with **avere**) | |

| | **potere** | **to be able** | **volere** | **to want** |
|---|---|---|---|---|
| (io) | **posso** | I can | **voglio** | I want |
| (tu) | **puoi** | you can | **vuoi** | you want |
| (lui/lei) | **può** | (s)he can | **vuole** | (s)he wants |
| (noi) | **possiamo** | we can | **vogliamo** | we want |
| (voi) | **potete** | you can | **volete** | you want |
| (loro) | **possono** | they can | **vogliono** | they want |
| | *past participle:* | | *past participle:* | |
| | **potuto** (with **avere**) | | **voluto** (with **avere**) | |

| | **dovere** | **to have to** (must) |
|---|---|---|
| (io) | **devo** | I must |
| (tu) | **devi** | you must |
| (lui/lei) | **deve** | he/she must |
| (noi) | **dobbiamo** | we must |
| (voi) | **dovete** | you must |
| (loro) | **devono** | they must |

*past participle:* **dovuto** (with **avere**)

# Past tense

To form the past tense combine the present tense of the verb **avere** – *to have* with the past participle of the verb, e.g.

**ho parlato** → I spoke/I have spoken
**ho venduto** → I sold/I have sold

Note: Not all verbs take **avere** (**ho**, **hai**, etc.) as their auxiliary verb, some take **essere** (**sono**, **sei**, etc.). These are mainly verbs of motion or staying, e.g. **andare** – *to go*, **stare** – *to be (located at)*:

**sono andato** → I went
**sono stato a Roma** → I was in Rome

When the auxiliary verb **essere** is used, the past participle (**andato**, **stato**) becomes an adjective and should agree with the subject of the verb, e.g.:

**sono andata** → I went (*fem. sing.*)
**siamo stati** → we went (*masc. plural*)

# Negative

To make a sentence negative, e.g. I am not eating, you use **non** before the verb.

**non mangio** → I am not eating
**non sono andato** → I did not go

# Public holidays

On national holidays you may find information offices closed, museums open for shorter hours and public transport running a limited service.

| | |
|---|---|
| January 1 | **Capodanno** New Year's Day |
| January 6 | **Epifania** Epiphany |
| March/April | **Pasquetta** Easter Monday |
| April 25 | **Anniversario della Liberazione** Liberation Day |
| May 1 | **Festa del Lavoro** Labour Day |
| June 2 | **Festa della Repubblica** Anniversary of the Founding of the Republic |
| August 15 | **Assunzione** Assumption |
| November 1 | **Ognissanti** All Saints |
| December 8 | **Immacolata Concezione** Immaculate Conception |
| December 25 | **Natale** Christmas Day |
| December 26 | **Santo Stefano** St Stephen's Day (Boxing Day) |

As well as the above national holidays, each town celebrates the feast-day of its patron saint, which differs from town to town.

# English – Italian



## A

| English | Italian | Pronunciation |
|---|---|---|
| **a(n)** | un/una/uno | oon/**oon**a/**oon**o |
| **able:** ***to be able (to)*** | essere capace (di) | **es**-seray ka-**pat**-chay (dee) |
| **about** | su; circa | soo; **cheer**-ka |
| **above** | sopra | **so**pra |
| **abroad** | all'estero *m* | al-**les**-tero |
| **access** | l'accesso *m* | at-**ches**-so |
| **accident** | l'incidente *m* | eenchee-**den**tay |
| **accident & emergency department** | il pronto soccorso | **pron**to sok-**kor**so |
| **accommodation** | l'alloggio *m* | al-**lod**-jo |
| **to accompany** | accompagnare | ak-kompan-**yar**ay |
| **account** (bill) | il conto | **kon**to |
| (in bank) | il conto in banca | **kon**to een **ban**ka |
| **to ache** | fare male | **fa**ray **ma**lay |
| ***it aches*** | fa male | fa **ma**lay |
| **address** | l'indirizzo *m* | een-dee**reets**-so |
| ***what is the address?*** | qual è l'indirizzo? | kwal **e** leen-dee**reets**-so? |
| **admission charge/fee** | il biglietto d'ingresso | beel-**yayt**-to din-**grays**-so |
| **to admit** (to hospital) | ricoverare | ree-kovay-**rar**ay |
| **adult** | l'adulto(a) | a-**dool**to(a) |
| **to advise** | consigliare | konseel-**yar**ay |
| **A&E** | il pronto soccorso | **pron**to sok-**kor**so |
| **afraid:** ***to be afraid*** | avere paura | a-**vay**ray pa-**oo**ra |
| **after** | dopo | **do**po |
| **afternoon** | il pomeriggio | pomay-**reed**-jo |
| ***this afternoon*** | oggi pomeriggio | **od**jee pomay-**reed**-jo |
| ***tomorrow afternoon*** | domani pomeriggio | do-**ma**nee pomay-**reed**-jo |
| ***in the afternoon*** | di pomeriggio | dee pomay-**reed**-jo |
| **again** | ancora; di nuovo | an**kor**a; dee **nwo**-vo |
| **against** | contro | **kon**tro |

| | | |
|---|---|---|
| **age** | l'età *f* | e-**ta** |
| **ago** | fa | fa |
| **to agree** | essere d'accordo | **es**-seray dak-**kor**do |
| **agreement** | l'accordo *m* | ak-**kor**do |
| **air-conditioning** | l'aria condizionata *f* | **ar**ya kondeetsyo-**na**ta |
| **airplane** | l'aereo *m* | a-**ayr**ay-o |
| **airport** | l'aeroporto *m* | a-ayro-**por**to |
| **airport bus** | l'autobus per l'aeroporto *m* | **ow**-toboos payr la-ayro **por**to |
| **air ticket** | il biglietto d'aereo | beel-**yayt**- to **day**-rayo |
| **alarm** | l'allarme *m* | al-**lar**may |
| **alarm clock** | la sveglia | **svel**-ya |
| **alcohol** | l'alcool *m* | **al**-kol |
| **alcoholic** | alcolico(a) | al-**ko**leeko(a) |
| **all** | tutto(a) | **toot**-to(a) |
| **allergic to** | allergico(a) a | al-**ler**-jeeko(a) a |
| ***I'm allergic to...*** | sono allergico(a) a... | **so**no al-**ler**-jeeko(a) a... |
| **allergy** | l'allergia *f* | al-layr-**djee**a |
| **to allow** | permettere | per-**met**-tayray |
| **all right** (agreed) | va bene | va **be**nay |
| **almost** | quasi | **kwa**zee |
| **alone** | solo(a) | **so**lo(a) |
| **already** | già | dj**a** |
| **also** | anche | **an**kay |
| **always** | sempre | **sem**pray |
| **a.m.** | del mattino | del mat-**tee**no |
| **am:** ***I am*** | sono | **so**no |
| **ambulance** | l'ambulanza *f* | amboo-**lan**tsa |
| **American** | americano(a) | ameree-**ka**no(a) |
| **anaesthetic** | l'anestetico *m* | anes-**tay**teeko |
| **and** | e | ay |
| **angry** | arrabbiato(a) | ar-rab-**bya**to(a) |
| **to announce** | annunciare | an-noon-**tchee**-aray |
| **another** | un altro/un'altra | oon **al**tro/oon **al**tra |
| **answer** | la risposta | rees-**pos**ta |
| **to answer** | rispondere | rees-**pon**-dayray |

# English - Italian



| English | Italian | Pronunciation |
|---|---|---|
| **answering machine** | la segreteria telefonica | segretay-**ree**-a telay-**fon**-eeka |
| **antibiotic** | l'antibiotico *m* | anteebee-**ot**eeko |
| **antihistamine** | l'antistaminico | anteesta-**meen**eeko |
| **any** | dei/delle/degli (di) | day/**del**-lay/**del**-yee (dee) |
| ***I haven't any money*** | non ho soldi | non o **sol**dee |
| **anyone** | qualcuno; chiunque | kwal-**koo**no; kee-**oonk**-way |
| **anything** | qualcosa; qualsiasi cosa | kwal-**ko**za; kwal-**see**ya-see **ko**za |
| **apartment** | l'appartamento *m* | ap-parta-**mayn**to |
| **apple** | la mela | **may**la |
| **approximately** | circa | **cheer**-ka |
| **apricots** | le albicocche | albee-**kok**-kay |
| **arm** | il braccio | **brat**-cho |
| **to arrange** | sistemare | seestay-**mar**ay |
| **arrivals** (plane, train) | gli arrivi | ar-**ree**vee |
| **to arrive** | arrivare | ar-ree-**var**ay |
| **art** | l'arte *f* | **art**ay |
| **to ask** (question) | domandare | do-man-**dar**ay |
| (for something) | chiedere | **kee**-ederay |
| **asleep: *he/she is asleep*** | dorme | **dor**-may |
| **aspirin** | l'aspirina *f* | aspee-**ree**na |
| **asthma** | l'asma *f* | **az**-ma |
| ***I have asthma*** | ho l'asma | o l**az**-ma |
| **at** | a | a |
| ***at home*** | a casa | a **ka**za |
| ***at 8 o'clock*** | alle otto | al-**lay ot**-to |
| ***at once*** | subito | **soo**-beeto |
| ***at night*** | di notte | dee **not**-tay |
| **ATM** | il Bancomat® | **ban**komat |
| **to attack** | aggredire | ag-gray-**deer**ay |
| **attractive** | attraente | at-tra-**ent**ay |
| **automatic** | automatico(a) | owto-**ma**-teeko(a) |
| **autumn** | l'autunno *m* | ow**toon**-no |

| English | Italian | Pronunciation |
|---|---|---|
| **available** | disponibile | deespo-**nee**-beelay |
| **to avoid** | evitare | evee-**tar**-ay |
| **away** | via | **vee**-a |
| **awful** | terribile | ter-**ree**-beelay |

## B

| English | Italian | Pronunciation |
|---|---|---|
| **baby** | il/la bambino(a) | bam-**bee**no(a) |
| **baby milk** | il latte per bambini | **la**t-tay payr bam-**bee**nee |
| **baby seat** (in car) | il seggiolino per bambini | sed-djo-**lee**no payr bam-**bee**nee |
| **babysitter** | il/la babysitter | bay-bee-**sit**-ter |
| **baby wipes** | le salviettine per bambini | sal-vyet- **tee**nay payr bam-**bee**nee |
| **back** (of body) | la schiena | **skee**-ay-na |
| **bad** (weather, news) | brutto(a) | **broo**t-to(a) |
| (food) | andato(a) a male | an-**da**to(a) a **ma**lay |
| **bag** | la borsa | **bor**sa |
| **baggage** | i bagagli | ba**gal**-yee |
| **baker's** | la panetteria | panayt-tay-**ree**-a |
| **banana** | la banana | ba-**nan**a |
| **bank** | la banca | **ban**ka |
| (river) | la riva | **ree**va |
| **bank account** | il conto in banca | **kon**to een **ban**ka |
| **banknote** | la banconota | banko-**no**ta |
| **bar** | il bar | bar |
| **bath** | il bagno | **ban**-yo |
| **bathroom** | il bagno | **ban**-yo |
| ***with bathroom*** | con bagno | kon **ban**-yo |
| **battery** (radio) | la pila | **pee**la |
| **B&B** | la pensione familiare | pens-**yon**ay famee-**lyar**-ay |
| **to be** | essere | **es**-seray |
| **beach** | la spiaggia | **spee**-ad-ja |
| **bean** | il fagiolo | fa-**jo**lo |
| **beautiful** | bello(a) | **bel**-lo(a) |
| **because** | perché | per**kay** |
| **to become** | diventare | deeven-**tar**ay |

| | | |
|---|---|---|
| **bed** | il letto | **let**-to |
| ***double bed*** | il letto matrimoniale | **let**-to matree-mon-**ya**lay |
| ***single bed*** | il letto a una piazza | **let**-to a oona **pee**-at-tsa |
| **bed and breakfast** | la pensione familiare | pens-**yon**ay famee-**lyar**-ay |
| **bedroom** | la camera da letto | **kam**-ayra da **let**-to |
| **beer** | la birra | **beer**-ra |
| ***draught beer*** | la birra alla spina | **beer**-ra al-la **spee**na |
| **before** | prima di | **pree**ma dee |
| ***before breakfast*** | prima di colazione | **pree**ma dee kolats-**yon**ay |
| **to begin** | cominciare | komeen-**char**ay |
| **behind** | dietro | **dee**-etro |
| **to belong to** | appartenere a | ap-partay-**nayr**ay a |
| ***it belongs to...*** | appartiene a... | ap-par-**tyay**nay a... |
| **below** | sotto | **sot**-to |
| **beside** (next to) | accanto a | ak-**kan**to a |
| **best:** ***the best*** | il/la migliore | meel-**yor**ay |
| **better** (than) | meglio (di) | **mel**-yo (dee) |
| **between** | fra | fra |
| **beyond** | oltre | **ol**-tray |
| **bicycle** | la bicicletta | beechee-**klet**-ta |
| **big** | grande | **gran**day |
| **bigger** (than) | più grande (di) | pyoo **gran**day (dee) |
| **bill** (hotel, restaurant) | il conto | **kon**to |
| (for work done) | la fattura | fat-**too**ra |
| (gas, telephone) | la bolletta | bol-**let**-ta |
| **birthday** | il compleanno | komplay-**an**-no |
| ***happy birthday!*** | auguri! buon compleanno | ow-**goo**-ree! bwon komplay-**an**-no |
| **biscuits** | i biscotti | bees-**kot**-tee |
| **bit** | il pezzo | **pets**-so |
| ***a bit*** | un po' | oon po |

| | | |
|---|---|---|
| **bite** (of insect) | la puntura | poon-**toor**a |
| (of dog) | il morso | **mor**so |
| **to bite** (animal) | mordere | **mor**-deray |
| (insect) | pungere | poon-**jay**ray |
| **bitten** (by insect) | morso(a) | **mor**so(a) |
| | punto(a) | **poo**nto(a) |
| **bitter** (taste) | amaro(a) | a-**mar**o(a) |
| **black** | nero(a) | **ne**-ro(a) |
| **to bleed** | sanguinare | san-gwee-**nar**ay |
| **blind** (person) | cieco(a) | **chee**-ek-o(a) |
| **block of flats** | il palazzo | pa-**lat**-tso |
| **blond** (person) | biondo(a) | **byon**-do(a) |
| **blood** | il sangue | **san**-gway |
| **blood pressure** | la pressione sanguigna | pres-**syon**ay san-**gwee**-nya |
| **blood test** | l'analisi del sangue *f* | a-**nal**ee-zee del **san**-gway |
| **blouse** | la camicetta | kamee-**chet**-ta |
| **to blow-dry** | asciugare con il fon | ashyoo-**gar**ay kon eel fon |
| **blue** (light) | azzurro(a) | ad-**dzoo**r-ro(a) |
| **to board** (plane, train, etc) | imbarcarsi su | eembar-**kar**-see soo |
| **boarding card/pass** | la carta d'imbarco | **kar**ta deem-**bar**ko |
| **body** | il corpo | **kor**po |
| **to boil** | bollire | bol-**leer**ay |
| **book** | il libro | **lee**bro |
| **to book** | prenotare | preno-**tar**ay |
| **booking** | la prenotazione | prenotat-**tzyon**ay |
| **booking office** (train) | la biglietteria | beel-yet-tay-**ree**-a |
| **bookshop** | la libreria | leebray-**ree**-a |
| **boots** (long) | gli stivali | stee-**va**lee |
| **boring** | noioso(a) | no-**yo**-so(a) |
| **born: *to be born*** | essere nato(a) | **es**-seray **na**to(a) |
| **to borrow** | prendere in prestito | **pren**-deray een pres**tee**-to |
| **both** | tutti e due | **toot**-tee ay **doo**ay |
| **bottle** | la bottiglia | bot-**teel**-ya |

| | | |
|---|---|---|
| **box office** | il botteghino | bot-tay-**gee**no |
| **boy** (young child) | il bambino | bam-**bee**no |
| (teenage) | il ragazzo | ra-**gats**-so |
| **boyfriend** | il ragazzo | ra-**gats**-so |
| **to brake** | frenare | fray-**nar**ay |
| **brakes** | i freni | **fray**nee |
| **bread** | il pane | **pan**ay |
| ***brown bread*** | il pane integrale | **pan**ay eentay-**gra**lay |
| ***bread roll*** | il panino | pa-**nee**no |
| **to break** | rompere | **rom**-peray |
| **breakfast** | la (prima) colazione | (**pree**ma) kolats-**yon**ay |
| **breast** | il seno | **say**no |
| **to breathe** | respirare | res-pee-**rar**ay |
| **bride** | la sposa | **spo**za |
| **bridegroom** | lo sposo | **spo**zo |
| **briefcase** | la cartella | kar-**tel**-la |
| **to bring** | portare | por-**tar**ay |
| **Britain** | la Gran Bretagna | gran bray-**tan**ya |
| **British** | britannico(a) | bree-**tan**-neeko(a) |
| **brochure** | l'opuscolo *m* | o-**poos**kolo |
| **broken** | rotto(a) | **rot**-to(a) |
| **broken down** | guasto(a) | **gwas**-to(a) |
| **bronchitis** | la bronchite | bron-**kee**tay |
| **brother** | il fratello | fra-**tel**-lo |
| **brother-in-law** | il cognato | kon-**ya**to |
| **brown** | marrone | mar-**ron**-ay |
| **to build** | costruire | kostroo-**eer**ay |
| **bulb** (lightbulb) | la lampadina | lampa-**dee**na |
| **bureau de change** | l'agenzia di cambio *f* | adjen-**tsi**a dee kam-**byo** |
| **burger** | l'hamburger *m* | am-**boor**ger |
| **burglar** | il/la ladro(a) | **la**dro(a) |
| **bus** | l'autobus *m* | **ow**-toboos |
| **bus stop** | la fermata (dell'autobus) | fer-**mat**a (del-**low**-toboos) |
| **bus ticket** | il biglietto d'autobus | beel-**yet**-to d**ow**-toboos |
| **business** | gli affari | af-**far**ee |

| | | |
|---|---|---|
| **businessman/ woman** | l'uomo/la donna d'affari | **wo**mo/**don**-na daf-**far**ee |
| **business trip** | il viaggio d'affari | **vee**-ad-djo daf-**far**ee |
| **busy** | occupato(a); impegnato(a) | ok-koo-**pa**to(a); eem-pen-**ya**to(a) |
| **but** | ma; però | ma; pe-**ro** |
| **butter** | il burro | **boor**-ro |
| **to buy** | comprare | kom-**pra**ray |
| **by** (next to) | accanto a | ak-**kan**to a |
| ***by bus*** | in autobus | een **ow**-toboos |
| ***by car*** | in macchina | een **mak**-keena |
| ***by train*** | in treno | een **tray**no |

## C

| | | |
|---|---|---|
| **cab** (taxi) | il taxi | **tak**see |
| **café** | il bar | bar |
| **cafetière** | la caffettiera | kaf-fet-**tyer**a |
| **cake** (big) | la torta | **tor**ta |
| (small) | il pasticcino | pastee-**chee**no |
| **cake shop** | la pasticceria | pasteechay-**ree**-a |
| **call** (phone call) | la chiamata | kya-**mat**a |
| **to call** (phone) | chiamare | kya-**mar**ay |
| | chiamare per telefono | kya-**mar**ay payr te-**lef**ono |
| **camcorder** | la videocamera | veeday-o-**kam**ayra |
| **camera** | la macchina fotografica | **mak**-keena foto-**gra**-feeka |
| **to camp** | campeggiare | kamped-**jar**ay |
| **campsite** | il campeggio | kam-**ped**-jo |
| **can** (to be able) | potere | po-**tay**ray |
| ***I can*** | posso | **pos**-so |
| ***I cannot*** | non posso | non **pos**-so |
| ***can I...?*** | posso...? | **pos**-so...? |
| **to cancel** | annullare | an-nool-**lar**ay |
| **cancellation** | la cancellazione | kanchel-lats-**yon**ay |
| **car** | la macchina | **mak**-keena |
| **car alarm** | l'antifurto *m* | antee-**foor**to |
| **car hire** | l'autonoleggio *m* | owto-no-**led**-jo |

| English | Italian | Pronunciation |
|---|---|---|
| **car insurance** | l'assicurazione della macchina *f* | as-seekoorats-**yon**ay **del**-la **mak**-keena |
| **car keys** | le chiavi della macchina | **kee**-avee **del**-la **mak**-keena |
| **car park** | il parcheggio | par-**ked**-jo |
| **card** (greetings) | il biglietto d'auguri | beel-**yet**-to dow-**goo**-ree |
| (business) | il biglietto da visita | beel-**yet**-to da **vee**-zeeta |
| **careful** | attento(a) | at-**ten**to(a) |
| **carriage** (railway) | il vagone | va-**gon**ay |
| **carrots** | le carote | ka-**rot**ay |
| **to carry** | portare | por-**tar**ay |
| **case** (suitcase) | la valigia | va-**lee**ja |
| **cash** | i contanti | kon-**tan**tee |
| **to cash** (cheque) | incassare | eenkas-**sar**ay |
| **cash desk** | la cassa | **kas**-sa |
| **cash machine** | il Bancomat® | **ban**komat |
| **castle** | il castello | kas-**tel**-lo |

| English | Italian | Pronunciation |
|---|---|---|
| **casualty department** | il pronto soccorso | **pron**to sok-**kor**so |
| **cat** | il gatto | **gat**-to |
| **to catch** (train, etc) | prendere | **pren**-deray |
| **cathedral** | il duomo | **dwo**mo |
| **cauliflower** | il cavolfiore | kavolf-**yor**ay |
| **CD** | il CD | chee**dee** |
| **cellphone** | il cellulare | chel-loo-**lar**ay |
| **cent** (euro) | il centesimo | chen-**tay**zeemo |
| **centimetre** | il centimetro | chen-**tee**metro |
| **central** | centrale | chen-**tra**lay |
| **central heating** | il riscaldamento | reeskalda**men**to |
| **centre** | il centro | **chen**tro |
| **cereal** (for breakfast) | i cereali | cheray-**al**ee |
| **certificate** | il certificato | cherteefee-**kat**o |
| **chair** | la sedia | **sed**-ya |
| **change** | il cambio | kamb-**yo** |
| (small coins) | gli spiccioli | **speet**-cholee |
| (money returned) | il resto | **res**to |

| | | |
|---|---|---|
| **to change:** ***to change money*** | cambiare i soldi | kamb-**yar**ay ee **sol**dee |
| ***to change clothes*** | cambiarsi | kamb-**yar**see |
| ***to change trains*** | cambiare treno | kamb-**yar**ay **tray**no |
| **charge** (fee) | la tariffa | ta-**reef**-fa |
| **charge** (for mobile, etc) | la carica | **kar**eeka |
| ***to charge*** (mobile, etc) | (ri)caricare | (ree)-karee-**kar**ay |
| **to charge** | addebitare | ad-debee-**tar**ay |
| ***charge it to my account*** | lo metta sul mio conto | **met**-ta sool **mee**yo **kon**to |
| **cheap** | economico(a) | eko-**nom**eeko(a) |
| ***cheaper*** | più economico(a) | pyoo eko-**nom**eeko(a) |
| **to check** | controllare | kontrol-**lar**ay |
| **to check in** (airport) | fare il check-in | **fa**ray eel chek-**een** |
| (at hotel) | firmare il registro | feer-**mar**ay eel re-**jees**tro |
| **cheers!** | salute!; cin-cin! | sa-**loot**ay!; cheen-**cheen**! |
| **cheese** | il formaggio | for-**mad**-jo |
| **chemist's** | la farmacia | farma-**chee**ya |
| **cheque** | l'assegno *m* | as-**sen**-yo |
| **cheque book** | il libretto degli assegni | lee-**bret**-to **del**-yee as-**sen**-yee |
| **cheque card** | la carta assegni | **kar**ta as-**sen**-yee |
| **cherries** | le ciliegie | cheel-**ye**-jay |
| **chicken** | il pollo | **pol**-lo |
| **chicken breast** | il petto di pollo | **pet**-to dee **pol**-lo |
| **chilli** | il peperoncino | peperon-**cheen**o |
| **child** | il/la bambino(a) | bam-**been**o(a) |
| **children** (small) | i bambini | bam-**been**ee |
| (older children) | i ragazzi | ra-**gats**-see |
| **chips** (french fries) | le patatine fritte | pata-**teen**ay **free**-tay |
| **chocolate** | la cioccolata | chok-ko-**lat**a |

| English | Italian | Pronunciation |
|---|---|---|
| **chocolates** | i cioccolatini | chok-kola-**teen**ee |
| **to choose** | scegliere | **shel**-yeray |
| **Christmas** | il Natale | na-**tal**ay |
| **church** | la chiesa | kee-**e**za |
| **cigarette** | la sigaretta | seega-**ret**-ta |
| **cigarette lighter** | l'accendino | atchen-**dee**no |
| **cinema** | il cinema | **chee**-nayma |
| **city** | la città | cheet-**ta** |
| **city centre** | il centro città | **chen**tro cheet-**ta** |
| **class:** ***first class*** | prima classe | **pree**ma **klas**-say |
| ***second class*** | seconda classe | se-**kon**da **klas**-say |
| **clean** | pulito(a) | poo-**leet**o(a) |
| **to clean** | pulire | poo-**leer**ay |
| **clear** | chiaro(a) | kee-**a**-ro(a) |
| **client** | il/la cliente | klee-**ent**ay |
| **to climb** | scalare | ska-**lar**ay |
| **clock** | l'orologio *m* | oro-**loj**o |
| **to close** | chiudere | **kyoo**-deray |
| **closed** (shop, etc) | chiuso(a) | **kyoo**zo(a) |
| **clothes** | i vestiti | ves-**teet**ee |
| **clothes shop** | il negozio d'abbiglia-mento | ne-**gots**-yo dab-beelya-**ment**o |
| **cloudy** | nuvoloso(a) | noovo-**lo**so(a) |
| **coach** | il pullman | **pool**man |
| **coast** | la costa | **kos**ta |
| **coat** | il cappotto | kap-**pot**-to |
| **cocoa** | il cacao | kak-**ow** |
| **coffee** (espresso) | il caffè | kaf-**fe** |
| ***black coffee*** | il caffè americano | kaf-**fe** ameree-**kan**o |
| ***white coffee*** | il caffellatte | kaf-fel-**lat**-tay |
| ***instant coffee*** | il caffè solubile | kaf-**fe** so-**loo**-beelay |
| ***decaffeinated coffee*** | il decaffeinato | deekaf-fe-**nat**o |
| **coin** | la moneta | mo-**net**a |
| **Coke®** | la Coca® | **ko**ka |
| **cold** | freddo(a) | **fred**-do(a) |

| | | |
|---|---|---|
| **cold** (illness) | il raffreddore | raf-fred-**dor**ay |
| ***I have a cold*** | ho il raffreddore | o eel raf-fred-**dor**ay |
| **colleague** | il/la collega | kol-**le**ga |
| **colour** | il colore | ko-**lor**ay |
| **to come** | venire | ve-**neer**ay |
| (to arrive) | arrivare | ar-ree-**var**ay |
| **to come back** | tornare | tor-**nar**ay |
| **to come in** | entrare | en-**trar**ay |
| ***come in!*** | avanti! | a-**van**tee! |
| **comfortable** | comodo(a) | **kom**odo(a) |
| **company** (firm) | la ditta | **deet**-ta |
| **to complain** | fare un reclamo | **fa**ray oon re-**klam**o |
| **complaint** | il reclamo | re-**klam**o |
| **complete** | completo(a) | kom-**plet**o(a) |
| **computer** | il computer | kom-**pyoo**ter |
| **concert** | il concerto | kon-**cher**to |
| **conditioner** | il balsamo | **bal**samo |
| **condoms** | i preservativi | preserva-**tee**vee |
| **conference** | il congresso | kon-**gres**-so |
| **to confirm** | confermare | konfer-**mar**ay |
| **confirmation** (of flight, etc) | la conferma | kon-**ferm**a |
| **confused** | confuso(a) | kon-**foo**zo(a) |
| **congratulations** | le felicitazioni | fay-leechee-tats-**yon**ee |
| **connection** (train, etc) | la coincidenza | koeen-chee-**den**tsa |
| **consulate** | il consolato | konso-**lat**o |
| **to consult** | consultare | konsool-**tar**ay |
| **to contact** | mettersi in contatto con | **met**-tersee een kon-**tat**-to kon |
| **contact lenses** | le lenti a contatto | **lent**ee a kon-**tat**-to |
| **to continue** | continuare | konteenoo-**ar**ay |
| **contraceptive** | l'anticoncezionale | anteekonchets-yo-**na**-lay |
| **to cook** | cucinare | koo-tcheen-**ar**ay |
| **cooked** | cotto(a) | **kot**-to(a) |
| **cooker** | la cucina | koo-**tchee**na |
| **cookies** | i biscotti | bees-**kot**-tee |

| | | |
|---|---|---|
| **cool** | fresco(a) | **fres**ko(a) |
| **corner** | l'angolo *m* | **an**golo |
| **corridor** | il corridoio | kor-ree-**doy**o |
| **to cost** | costare | kos-**tar**ay |
| **costume** (swimming) | il costume da bagno | kos-**toom**ay da **ban**-yo |
| **cough** | la tosse | **tos**-say |
| **to cough** | tossire | tos-**seer**ay |
| **country** (not town) | la campagna | kam-**pan**ya |
| (nation) | il paese | pa-**ez**ay |
| **couple** (two people) | la coppia | **kop**-pya |
| **courgettes** | gli zucchini | tsook-**keen**ee |
| **course** (of meal) | il piatto | **pyat**-to |
| **cover charge** | il coperto | ko-**per**to |
| **crash** (car) | lo scontro | **skon**tro |
| **to crash** (car) | avere un incidente | a-**vay**ray oon eenchee-**dent**ay |
| **cream** (lotion) | la crema | **krem**a |
| (dairy) | la panna | **pan**-na |
| **credit card** | la carta di credito | **kar**ta dee **kray**-deeto |
| **crisps** | le patatine | pata-**teen**ay |
| **crossroads** | l'incrocio *m* | een-**kroch**o |
| **cucumber** | il cetriolo | chetree-**ol**o |
| **cup** | la tazza | **tat**-tsa |
| **customer** | il/la cliente | klee-**ent**ay |
| **customs** (duty) | la dogana | do-**gan**a |
| **to cut** | tagliare | tal-**yar**ay |
| **to cycle** | andare in bicicletta | an-**dar**ay een beechee-**klet**-ta |
| **cystitis** | la cistite | chis-**teet**ay |

## D

| | | |
|---|---|---|
| **damage** | il danno | **dan**-no |
| **to dance** | ballare | bal-**lar**ay |
| **dangerous** | pericoloso(a) | pereeko-**los**o(a) |
| **dark** (colour) | scuro(a) | **skoo**ro(a) |
| **date** | la data | **da**ta |
| **date of birth** | la data di nascita | **da**ta dee **nash**eeta |

| English | Italian | Pronunciation |
|---|---|---|
| **daughter** | la figlia | **feel**-ya |
| **day** | il giorno | **jor**no |
| ***per day*** | al giorno | al **jor**no |
| **deaf** | sordo(a) | **sor**do(a) |
| **debit card** | la carta di addebito | **kar**ta dee ad-**deb**eeto |
| **decaffeinated** | decaffeinato(a) | deekaf-fe-**nat**o(a) |
| **delay** | il ritardo | ree-**tar**do |
| **delayed: *to be delayed*** (flight) | subire un ritardo | soo-**beer**ay oon ree-**tar**do |
| **dentist** | il/la dentista | den-**tee**sta |
| **to depart** | partire | par-**teer**ay |
| **department store** | il grande magazzino | **gran**day magad-**zeen**o |
| **departure** | la partenza | par-**tent**sa |
| **departure lounge** | la sala partenze | **sa**la par-**tent**say |
| **dessert** | il dolce | **dol**chay |
| **diabetic** | diabetico(a) | deea-**be**-teeko(a) |
| ***I'm diabetic*** | sono diabetico(a) | **son**o deea-**be**-teeko(a) |
| **to dial** | fare il numero | **fa**ray eel **noo**-mayro |
| **dialling code** | il prefisso telefonico | pre-**fees**-so tele-**fon**eeko |
| **diesel** | il gasolio | ga-**zol**yo |
| **diet** | la dieta | dee-**ye**ta |
| ***I'm on a diet*** | sono a dieta | **son**o a dee-**ye**ta |
| **different** | diverso(a) | dee-**vers**o(a) |
| **difficult** | difficile | deef-**fee**-cheelay |
| **digital camera** | la fotocamera digitale | foto-**ka**-mayra deejee-**tal**ay |
| **dining room** | la sala da pranzo | **sal**a da **pran**tso |
| **dinner** (evening meal) | la cena | **chay**na |
| ***to have dinner*** | cenare | chay-**nar**ay |
| **directions** | le indicazioni | eendeekatz-**yon**ee |
| **dirty** | sporco(a) | **spor**ko(a) |
| **disabled** (person) | disabile | dee-**zab**eelay |
| **disco** | la discoteca | deesko-**tek**a |

| English | Italian | Pronunciation |
|---|---|---|
| **discount** | lo sconto | **skon**to |
| **disease** | la malattia | malat-**tee**-a |
| **disposable** (camera) | usa e getta | **oos**a ay **jet**-ta |
| **distance** | la distanza | dees-**tant**sa |
| **to disturb** | disturbare | deestoor-**bar**ay |
| **diversion** | la deviazione | deevee-ats-**yon**ay |
| **divorced** | divorziato(a) | deevorts-**yat**o(a) |
| **dizzy: *to be dizzy*** | avere capogiri | a-**vay**ray kapo-**jeer**ee |
| **to do** | fare | **fa**ray |
| **doctor** | il medico | **med**eeko |
| **documents** | i documenti | dokoo-**ment**ee |
| **dog** | il cane | **kan**ay |
| **dollars** | i dollari | **dol**-laree |
| **domestic** (flight) | nazionale | nats-yo-**nal**ay |
| **door** | la porta | **port**a |
| **double** | doppio(a) | **dop**-pyo(a) |
| **double bed** | il letto matrimoniale | **let**-to matree-mon-**yal**ay |
| **double room** | la camera doppia | **ka**-mayra **dop**-pya |
| **down: *to go down*** | scendere | **shen**-deray |
| **downstairs** | giù | joo |
| **draught lager** | la birra alla spina | **beer**-ra al-la **spee**na |
| **dress** | il vestito | ves-**teet**o |
| **dressing** (for food) | il condimento | kondee-**ment**o |
| **drink** (soft) | la bibita | **bee**-beeta |
| **to drink** | bere | **ber**ay |
| **drinking water** | l'acqua potabile *f* | **ak**wa po-**ta**beelay |
| **to drive** | guidare | gwee-**dar**ay |
| **driver** (of car) | l'autista (*m/f*) | ow-**tees**ta |
| **driving licence** | la patente | pa-**ten**-tay |
| **drug** (medicine) | il farmaco | **farm**-ako |
| **drunk** | ubriaco(a) | oobree-**ak**o(a) |
| **dry** | secco(a); asciutto(a) | **sek**-ko(a); a-**shoot**-to(a) |

**dry-cleaner's** la tintoria teento-**ree**ya
**during** durante doo-**rant**ay
**duty-free** esente da dogana e-**zen**tay da do-**gan**a
**DVD player** il lettore DVD let-**tor**ay dee-voo-**dee**

## E

**each** ogni **on**-yee
**ear** l'orecchio *m* o**rek**-yo
**earache** il mal d'orecchi mal do**rek**-ee
**earlier** più presto pyoo **pres**to
**early** presto **pres**to
**to earn** guadagnare gwadan-**yar**ay
**east** l'est *m* est
**easy** facile **fach**eelay
**to eat** mangiare man-**jar**ay
**egg** l'uovo *m* **wo**vo
***eggs*** le uova **wo**va
**Elastoplast** il cerotto chay-**rot**-to
**electric** elettrico(a) e-**let**-treeko(a)
**electricity** l'elettricità *f* elet-treechee-**ta**
**electronic** elettronico(a) elet-**tron**-eeko(a)
**e-mail** la posta elettronica; l'e-mail *f* **pos**ta elet-**tron**-eeka; ee-**mail**
***to e-mail s.o.*** mandare e-mail man-**dar**ay ee-**mail**
**e-mail address** l'indirizzo e-mail eendee-**reet**-so ee-**mail**
**embassy** l'ambasciata *f* ambash-**ya**ta
**emergency** l'emergenza *f* emer-**jent**sa
**emergency exit** l'uscita d'emergenza *f* oo-**shee**ta demer-**jent**sa
**empty** vuoto(a) **vwo**to(a)
**end** la fine **feen**ay
**engaged** (to be married) fidanzato(a) feedan-**tsa**to(a)
(phone, toilet, etc) occupato(a) ok-koo-**pat**o(a)
**England** l'Inghilterra *f* een-geel-**ter**-ra

| | | |
|---|---|---|
| **English** (language) | inglese | een-**glay**say |
| | l'inglese *m* | een-**glay**say |
| **to enjoy** | divertirsi | deever-**teer**see |
| (to like) | piacere | pee-a-**chay**ray |
| **enough** | abbastanza | ab-bas-**tan**tsa |
| ***that's enough*** | basta così | **bas**ta ko-**zee** |
| **to enter** | entrare | en-**trar**ay |
| **entrance** | l'entrata *f*; l'ingresso *m* | en-**trat**a; een-**grays**-so |
| **entrance fee** | il biglietto d'ingresso | beel-**yet**-to deen-**grays**-so |
| **euro** | l'euro *m* | **ay**-oo-ro |
| **euro cent** | il centesimo | chen-**tay**zeemo |
| **evening** | la sera | **say**ra |
| ***this evening*** | stasera | sta-**say**ra |
| ***tomorrow evening*** | domani sera | do-**ma**nee **say**ra |
| **every** | ogni; ciascuno; tutti | **on**-yee; chee-as-**koo**no; **toot**-tee |
| **everyone** | tutti | **toot**-tee |
| **everything** | tutto | **toot**-to |
| **everywhere** | dappertutto | dap-per-**toot**-to |
| **excellent** | ottimo(a) | **ot**-teemo(a) |
| **except** | salvo | **sal**vo |
| **to exchange** | cambiare | kamb-**yar**ay |
| **exchange rate** | il cambio | kamb-**yo** |
| **exciting** | emozionante | emots-yo-**nan**tay |
| **excuse me!** (sorry) | mi scusi! | mee **skoo**zee! |
| (when passing) | permesso! | per-**mes**-so! |
| **exercise** | l'esercizio *m* | ezer-**cheets**-yo |
| **exhibition** | la mostra | **mos**tra |
| **exit** | l'uscita *f* | oo-**shee**ta |
| **expenses** | le spese | **spayz**ay |
| **expensive** | caro(a) | **ka**ro(a) |
| **to explain** | spiegare | spyay-**gar**ay |
| **to export** | esportare | espor-**tar**ay |
| **express** (train) | l'espresso *m* | es-**pres**-so |
| **extra** (spare) | in più | een pyoo |

| | | |
|---|---|---|
| (more) | supplementare | soop-play-men-**tar**ay |
| **eye** | l'occhio *m* | **ok**-yo |

## F

| | | |
|---|---|---|
| **face** | la faccia | **fat**-cha |
| **facilities** (leisure facilities) | le attrezzature | at-tret-tsa-**toor**ay |
| **to faint** | svenire | zve-**neer**ay |
| **fake** | falso(a) | **fals**o(a) |
| **to fall** | cadere | ka-**day**rey |
| **family** | la famiglia | fa-**meel**-ya |
| **far** | lontano(a) | lon-**tan**o(a) |
| **fare** | la tariffa | ta-**reef**-a |
| **fast** | veloce | vel-**och**ay |
| **to fasten** (seatbelt, etc) | allacciare | al-lat-**char**ay |
| **fat** | grasso(a) | **gras**-so(a) |
| **father** | il padre | **pad**ray |
| **fault** (defect) | il difetto | dee-**fet**-to |
| **favour** | il favore | fa-**vor**ay |
| **fax** | il fax | fax |
| **to fax** | mandare un fax | man-**dar**ay oon fax |
| **to feel** | sentire; sentirsi | sen-**teer**ay; sen-**teer**see |
| ***I don't feel well*** | non mi sento bene | non mee **sent**o **ben**ay |
| **feet** | i piedi | **pyed**ee |
| **fever** | la febbre | **feb**-bray |
| **few** | pochi | **po**-kee |
| ***a few*** | alcuni | al-**koon**ee |
| **fiancé(e)** | il/la fidanzato(a) | feedan-**tsa**to(a) |
| **to fill** | riempire | ree-em-**peer**ay |
| **to fill in** (form) | compilare | kompee-**lar**ay |
| **fillet** | il filetto | fee-**let**-to |
| **film** (at cinema) | il film | **feel**m |
| **to find** | trovare | tro-**var**ay |
| **fine** (to be paid) | la multa | **mool**ta |
| **finger** | il dito | **deet**o |
| **to finish** | finire | fee-**neer**ay |
| **finished** | finito(a) | fee-**neet**o(a) |

| English | Italian | Pronunciation |
|---|---|---|
| **fire** | il fuoco; l'incendio *m* | **fwo**ko; een-**chend**-yo |
| **fire alarm** | l'allarme antincendio *m* | al-**lar**may anteen-**chend**-yo |
| **fire escape** | la scala antincendio | **ska**la anteen-**chend**-yo |
| **fire extinguisher** | l'estintore | esteen-**tor**ay |
| **firm** (company) | l'azienda *f*; la ditta | adz-**yen**da; **deet**-ta |
| **first** | primo(a) | **pree**mo(a) |
| **first aid** | il pronto soccorso | **pron**to sok-**kor**so |
| **first class** | la prima classe | **pree**ma **klas**-say |
| **first name** | il nome di battesimo | **no**may dee bat-**tez**-eemo |
| **fish** | il pesce | **pesh**ay |
| **to fit** (clothes) | andare bene | an-**dar**ay **be**nay |
| ***it doesn't fit*** | non va bene | non va **be**nay |
| **fit** (seizure) | l'attacco *m* | at-**tak**-ko |
| **to fix** | riparare; sistemare | reepa-**rar**ay; sees-te-**ma**ray |
| **fizzy** | gassato(a) | gas-**sa**to(a) |
| **flash** (for camera) | il flash | flaysh |
| **flat** | l'appartamento *m* | ap-parta-**ment**o |
| **flat** | piatto(a) | **pyat**-to(a) |
| **flesh** | la carne | **kar**-nay |
| **flight** | il volo | **vol**o |
| **floor** (of building) | il piano | **pyan**o |
| (of room) | il pavimento | pavee-**ment**o |
| **flowers** | i fiori | **fyor**ee |
| **flu** | l'influenza *f* | eenfloo-**ent**za |
| **to fly** | volare | vo-**lar**ay |
| **fog** | la nebbia | **neb**-bya |
| **foggy** | nebbioso(a) | neb-**byo**so(a) |
| **food** | il cibo | **chee**bo |
| **food poisoning** | l'intossicazione alimentare *f* | een-tossee-cats-**yon**ay alee-men-**tar**ay |

| | | |
|---|---|---|
| **foot** | il piede | **pyed**ay |
| ***on foot*** | a piedi | a **pyed**ee |
| **football** | il calcio | **kal**-cho |
| **for** | per | payr |
| ***for me/us*** | per me/noi | payr may/noy |
| ***for him/her*** | per lui/lei | payr **loo**-ee/lay |
| ***for you*** | per te/lei/voi | payr tay/lay/voy |
| **forbidden** | proibito(a) | pro-ee-**beet**o(a) |
| **foreign** | straniero(a) | stran-**yayr**o(a) |
| **foreigner** | lo/la straniero(a) | stran-**yayr**o(a) |
| **forever** | per sempre | payr **semp**ray |
| **to forget** | dimenticare | deementee-**kar**ay |
| **fork** (for eating) | la forchetta | for-**ket**-ta |
| **form** (document) | il modulo | **mod**-oolo |
| **fortnight** | quindici giorni | **kween**-deechee **jor**nee |
| **forward** | avanti | a-**van**tee |
| **fracture** | la frattura | frat-**toor**a |
| **fragile** | fragile | **fraj**eelay |
| **free** (not occupied) | libero(a) | **lee**-bero(a) |
| (costing nothing) | gratis | **gra**tees |
| **French fries** | le patatine fritte | pata-**teen**ay **freet**-tay |
| **frequent** | frequente | fre-**kwen**tay |
| **fresh** | fresco(a) | **fres**ko(a) |
| **fried** | fritto(a) | **freet**-to(a) |
| **friend** | l'amico(a) | a-**mee**ko(a) |
| **from** | da | da |
| ***from England*** | dall'Inghilterra | dal-leen-geel-**ter**-ra |
| **front:** ***in front of...*** | davanti a... | da-**van**tee a... |
| **fruit** | la frutta | **froot**-ta |
| **fruit juice** | il succo di frutta | **sook**-ko dee **froot**-ta |
| **to fry** | friggere | **frid**-jeray |
| **fuel** (petrol) | la benzina | bend-**zeen**a |
| **full** | pieno(a) | **pyen**o(a) |
| (occupied) | completo(a) | kom-**play**-to(a) |

| | | |
|---|---|---|
| **full board** | la pensione completa | pens-**yon**ay kom-**play**-ta |
| **fun** | il divertimento | deevertee-**ment**o |
| **funny** (amusing) | divertente | deever-**tent**ay |

## G

| | | |
|---|---|---|
| **gallery** | la galleria | gal-lay-**ree**ya |
| **garden** | il giardino | jar-**dee**-no |
| **gate** (airport) | l'uscita *f* | oo-**shee**ta |
| **gay** (person) | gay | gey |
| **gents'** (toilet) | la toilette (per uomini) | twa-**let** (payr **wo**-meenee) |
| **to get** (obtain) | ottenere | ot-tay-**ner**ay |
| (to receive) | ricevere | ree-**chay**-veray |
| (to fetch) | prendere | **pren**-deray |
| ***to get in/on*** (vehicle) | salire in/su | sa-**leer**ay een/soo |
| ***to get off*** (bus, etc) | scendere da | **shen**-deray da |
| **gift** | il regalo | ray-**gal**o |
| **gift shop** | il negozio di souvenir | ne-**gots**-yo dee soovay-**neer** |
| **girl** (young child) | la bambina | bam-**bee**na |
| (teenage) | la ragazza | ra-**gats**-sa |
| **girlfriend** | la ragazza | ra-**gats**-sa |
| **to give** | dare | **dar**ay |
| **to give back** | restituire | resteetoo-**eer**ay |
| **glass** (substance) | il vetro | **vay**tro |
| (for drinking) | il bicchiere | beek-**yer**ay |
| **glasses** (specs) | gli occhiali | ok-**yal**ee |
| **to go** | andare | an-**dar**ay |
| ***to go back*** | ritornare | reetor-**nar**ay |
| **to go in** | entrare in | en-**trar**ay een |
| **to go out** (leave) | uscire | oo-**sheer**ay |
| **good** | buono(a) | **bwon**o(a) |
| (pleasant) | bello(a) | **bel**-lo(a) |
| ***very good*** | ottimo(a) | **ot**-teemo(a) |
| **good afternoon** | buon giorno | bwon **jor**no |
| (after 5pm) | buona sera | **bwon**a **say**ra |
| **goodbye** | arrivederci | ar-reevay-**der**chee |

| | | |
|---|---|---|
| **good evening** | buona sera | **bwon**a **say**ra |
| **good morning** | buon giorno | bwon **jor**no |
| **good night** | buona notte | **bwon**a **not**-tay |
| **gram** | il grammo | **gram**-mo |
| **grandchild** | il/la nipote | nee-**po**tay |
| **grandparents** | i nonni | **non**-nee |
| **grapefruit** | il pompelmo | pom-**pel**mo |
| **grapes** | l'uva *f* | **oov**a |
| **great** (big) | grande | **gran**-day |
| (wonderful) | fantastico(a) | fan-**tas**teeko(a) |
| **Great Britain** | la Gran Bretagna | gran-bray-**tan**-ya |
| **greengrocer's** | il fruttivendolo | froot-tee-**ven**-dolo |
| **grey** | grigio(a) | **gree**-jo(a) |
| **grilled** | alla griglia | **al**-la **greel**-ya |
| **grocer's** | il negozio di alimentari | ne-**gots**-yo dee alee-men-**tar**ee |
| **ground floor** | il pianterreno | pyanter-**ray**no |
| **group** | il gruppo | **groop**-po |
| **guesthouse** | la pensione | pens-**yon**ay |
| **guide** (tourist) | la guida | **gwee**-da |
| **guidebook** | la guida | **gwee**-da |
| **guided tour** | la visita guidata | **vee**-zeeta gwee-**dat**a |

## H

| | | |
|---|---|---|
| **hair** | i capelli | ka-**pel**-lee |
| **hairdresser** | il parrucchiere/ la parrucchiera | par-rook-**yer**ay/par-rook-**yer**a |
| **half** | la metà | me-**ta** |
| ***a half bottle of...*** | mezza bottiglia di... | **medz**-za bot-**teel**-ya dee... |
| ***half an hour*** | mezz'ora | medz-**zor**a |
| ***half board*** | mezza pensione | **medz**-za pens-**yon**ay |
| ***half-price*** | metà prezzo | me-**ta prets**-so |
| **ham** (cooked) | il prosciutto cotto | pro-**shoot**-to **kot**-to |
| (cured) | il prosciutto crudo | pro-**shoot**-to **kroo**-do |

| | | |
|---|---|---|
| **hand** | la mano | **ma**no |
| **handbag** | la borsa | **bor**sa |
| **handicapped** | disabile | dee-**zab**eelay |
| **handkerchief** | il fazzoletto | fats-so-**let**-to |
| **hand luggage** | il bagaglio a mano | ba**gal**-yo a **ma**no |
| **hand-made** | fatto(a) a mano | **fat**-to(a) a **ma**no |
| **hands-free kit** (for phone) | il vivavoce | veeva-**voch**ay |
| **to happen** | succedere | soot-**ched**-eray |
| ***what happened?*** | cos'è successo? | ko-ze soot-**ches**-so? |
| **happy** | felice | fe-**leech**ay |
| **hard** | duro(a) | **door**o(a) |
| (difficult) | difficile | deef-**fee**-cheelay |
| **to have** | avere | a-**vay**ray |
| ***I have...*** | ho... | o |
| ***I don't have...*** | non ho... | non o |
| ***do you have...?*** | ha/hai/avete...? | a/**a**-ee/a-**vay**tay? |
| **to have to** | dovere | do-**vay**ray |

| | | |
|---|---|---|
| **he** | lui | **loo**-ee |
| **head** | la testa | **test**a |
| **headache** | il mal di testa | mal dee **test**a |
| ***I have a headache*** | ho mal di testa | o mal dee **test**a |
| **health** | la salute | sa-**loot**ay |
| **health-food shop** | l'erboristeria *f* | erbo-reestay-**ree**-a |
| **healthy** | sano(a) | **sa**no(a) |
| **to hear** | sentire | sen-**teer**ay |
| **heart** | il cuore | **kwor**ay |
| **heating** | il riscaldamento | ree-skalda-**ment**o |
| **heavy** | pesante | pay-**sant**ay |
| **height** | l'altezza *f* | al-**tet**-tsa |
| **hello!** | salve!; ciao! | **sal**vay!; chow! |
| (on telephone) | pronto | **pron**to |
| **help!** | aiuto! | a-**yoo**to! |
| **to help** | aiutare | a-yoo-**tar**ay |
| ***can you help me?*** | può aiutarmi? | pwo a-yoo-**tar**mee? |
| **her** | il/la suo(a) | **soo**-o(a) |

| English | Italian | Pronunciation |
|---|---|---|
| **here** | qui/qua | kwee/kwa |
| ***here is...*** | ecco... | **ek**-ko... |
| **hi!** | ciao! | chow! |
| **to hide** | nascondere | nas-**kon**-deray |
| **high** | alto(a) | **al**to(a) |
| (speed) | forte | **for**tay |
| **him** | lui; lo; gli | **loo**-ee; lo; lyee |
| **hire** | il noleggio | no-**led**-jo |
| ***car hire*** | il noleggio auto | eel no-**led**-jo **ow**to |
| **to hire** | noleggiare | no-led-**jar**ay |
| **hired car** | la macchina a noleggio | **mak**-keena a no-**led**-jo |
| **his** | il/la suo(a) | **soo**-o(a) |
| **historic** | storico(a) | **stor**eeko(a) |
| **to hold** | tenere | tay-**ner**ay |
| (to contain) | contenere | kontay-**ner**ay |
| **holiday** | la festa | **fes**ta |
| ***on holiday*** | in vacanza | een va-**kant**sa |
| **home** | la casa | **kaz**a |
| ***at home*** | a casa | a **kaz**a |

| English | Italian | Pronunciation |
|---|---|---|
| **homosexual** | omosessuale | omo-ses-soo-**al**ay |
| **hors d'œuvre** | l'antipasto *m* | antee-**pas**to |
| **hospital** | l'ospedale *m* | ospay-**dal**ay |
| **hot** | caldo(a) | **kal**do(a) |
| **hotel** | l'albergo *m*; l'hotel *m* | al-**ber**go; o-**tel** |
| **hour** | l'ora *f* | **or**a |
| ***half an hour*** | mezz'ora | medz-**zor**a |
| ***1 hour*** | un'ora | oon-**or**a |
| ***2 hours*** | due ore | **doo**ay **or**ay |
| **house** | la casa | **kaz**a |
| **how?** | come? | **kom**ay? |
| ***how much?*** | quanto(a)? | **kwan**to(a)? |
| ***how many?*** | quanti(e)? | **kwan**tee(ay)? |
| ***how are you?*** | come sta? | **kom**ay sta? |
| **hungry:** ***to be hungry*** | avere fame | a-**vay**ray **fa**may |
| **hurry:** ***I'm in a hurry*** | ho fretta | o **fret**-ta |
| **to hurt** | fare male | **fa**ray **ma**lay |

***that hurts*** fa male fa **ma**lay
**husband** il marito ma-**ree**to

## I

**I** io **ee**-o
**ice** il ghiaccio **gyat**-cho
**ice cream** il gelato jay-**lat**o
**iced coffee** il caffè freddo kaf-**fe fred**-do
**ice lolly** il ghiacciolo gyat-**cho**lo
**identity card** la carta d'identità **kar**ta deedentee-**ta**
**if** se say
**ill** malato(a) ma-**lat**o(a)
***I'm ill*** sto male sto **ma**lay
**illness** la malattia malat-**tee**ya
**immediately** subito **soo**-beeto
**to import** importare eempor-**tar**ay
**important** importante eempor-**tant**ay
**impossible** impossibile eempos-**see**beelay
**to improve** migliorare meelyo-**rar**ay
**in** in een
***in front of*** davanti a da-**van**tee a
**included** compreso(a) kom-**pray**zo(a)
**inconvenient** scomodo(a) **sko**-modo(a)
**indigestion** l'indigestione *f* eendeejest-**yon**ay
**indoors** dentro **den**tro
**infection** l'infezione *f* eenfetz-**yon**ay
**informal** (clothes) sportivo(a) spor-**teev**o(a)
**information** le informazioni eenformats-**yon**ee
**ingredients** gli ingredienti eengray-**dyen**tee
**to injure** ferire fay-**reer**ay
**injured** ferito(a) fay-**reet**o(a)
**inquiries** le informazioni eenformats-**yon**ee
**insect** l'insetto *m* een-**set**-to
**inside** dentro **den**tro
**instant coffee** il caffè solubile ka-**fe** so-**loo**-beelay

| | | |
|---|---|---|
| **instead of** | invece di | een-**vech**ay dee |
| **insurance** | l'assicurazione *f* | as-seekoorats-**yon**ay |
| **to insure** | assicurare | as-seekoo-**rar**ay |
| **insured:** ***to be insured*** | essere assicurato(a) | **es**-seray as-seekoo-**rat**o(a) |
| **interesting** | interessante | eenteres-**sant**ay |
| **international** | internazionale | eenternats-yo-**nal**ay |
| **into** | in | een |
| ***into the centre*** | in centro | een **chen**tro |
| **to introduce someone to** | presentare qualcuno a | prezen-**tar**ay kwal-**koon**o a |
| **invitation** | l'invito *m* | een-**veet**o |
| **to invite** | invitare | eenvee-**tar**ay |
| **iron** (for clothes) | il ferro da stiro | **fer**-ro da **steer**o |
| **is** | è | e |
| **island** | l'isola *f* | **eez**ola |
| **it** | esso/essa; lo/la | **es**-so/**es**-sa; lo/la |
| **to itch** | prudere | **proo**-deray |

## J

| | | |
|---|---|---|
| **jacket** | la giacca | **jak**-ka |
| **jam** (food) | la marmellata | marmel-**lat**a |
| **jeans** | i blue jeans | bloo-**jins** |
| **jeweller's** | la gioielleria | jo-yel-lay-**ree**-a |
| **jewellery** | i gioielli | jo-**yel**-lee |
| **job** | il lavoro | la-**vor**o |
| **journalist** | il/la giornalista | jorna-**leest**a |
| **journey** | il viaggio | vee-**ad**-jo |
| **juice** | il succo | **sook**-ko |
| **just:** ***just two*** | solamente due | sola-**ment**ay **doo**ay |
| ***I've just arrived*** | sono appena arrivato(a) | **son**o ap-**pay**na ar-ree-**vat**o(a) |

## K

| | | |
|---|---|---|
| **keep the change!** | tenga il resto! | **ten**ga eel **rest**o! |
| **key** | la chiave | **kee**-avay |
| ***card key*** | il passe-partout | paspar-**too** |
| **kilo** | il chilo | **keel**o |

| | | |
|---|---|---|
| **kilometre** | il chilometro | kee-**lo**metro |
| **kind** (sort) | il tipo | **tee**po |
| **kind** (person) | gentile | jen-**teel**ay |
| **kiosk** | l'edicola *f* | ay-**deek**ola |
| **to knock** (on door) | bussare | boos-**sar**ay |
| **to know** (facts) | sapere | sa-**payr**ay |
| (person/place) | conoscere | ko-**nosh**eray |
| ***I don't know*** | non lo so | non lo so |
| **to know how to** | sapere | sa-**payr**ay |

## L

| | | |
|---|---|---|
| **ladies'** (toilet) | la toilette (per signore) | twa-**let** (payr see-**nyo**ray) |
| **lady** | la signora | see-**nyo**ra |
| **lager** | la birra (bionda) | **beer**-ra (bee-**on**da) |
| **lamb** | l'agnello *m* | la-**nyel**-lo |
| **to land** (plane) | atterrare | at-tayr-**ra**re |
| **language** | la lingua | **leen**-**gooa** |
| **large** | grande | **gran**-day |
| **last** | ultimo(a); scorso(a) | **ool**-teemo(a); **skor**-so(a) |
| ***last night*** | ieri sera | y**ay**-ree **say**-ra |
| ***last week*** | la settimana scorsa | sayt-tee**ma**na **skor**-sa |
| ***last year*** | l'anno scorso | **an**-no **skor**-so |
| **late** | tardi | **tar**-dee |
| ***later*** | più tardi | pee**oo tar**-dee |
| **lavatory** | la toilette | twa-**let** |
| **laxative** | il lassativo | las-sa**tee**vo |
| **lazy** | pigro(a) | **pee**gro(a) |
| **leather** | il cuoio; la pelle | koo-**o**-yo; **payl**-lay |
| **to leave** (leave behind) | lasciare | la**shya**ray |
| (train, bus, etc) | partire | par-**tee**ray |
| **left** | la sinistra | see**nee**stra |
| ***on/to the left*** | a sinistra | a see**nee**stra |
| **left-luggage** | il deposito bagagli | de**po**zeeto ba**ga**-lyee |

| | | |
|---|---|---|
| **leg** | la gamba | **gam**-ba |
| **lemon** | il limone | lee**mo**nay |
| **to lend** | prestare | pray-**sta**ray |
| **length** | la lunghezza | loon**gayt**-sa |
| **lens** (camera) | l'obiettivo *m* | obyet-**tee**vo |
| (contact lens) | la lente a contatto | **layn**-tay a con-**tat**-to |
| **less** | meno | **may**-no |
| ***less than*** | meno di | **may**-no dee |
| **to let** (allow) | permettere | per**mayt**-tayray |
| (to hire out) | affittare | af-feet-**ta**-ray |
| **letter** | la lettera | **let**-tayra |
| **licence** | il permesso | per-**mes**-so |
| (driving) | la patente | pa**ten**-tay |
| **to lie down** | sdraiarsi | zdra-**yar**see |
| **lift** (elevator) | l'ascensore *m* | ashen-**so**ray |
| **light** (not heavy) | leggero(a) | layd-**je**ro(a) |
| (colour) | chiaro(a) | kee**a**ro |
| **light** | la luce | **loo**chay |
| **like** | come | **ko**may |
| **to like** | piacere | pee-a-**chay**ray |
| ***I like coffee*** | mi piace il caffè | mee pee-**a**chay eel kaf-**fay** |
| ***I don't like...*** | non mi piace... | non mee pee**a**chay... |
| ***I'd/we'd like...*** | vorrei/ vorremmo... | vor-**ray**ee/ vor-**raym**-mo... |
| **line** (row, queue) | la fila | **fee**la |
| (telephone) | la linea | **leen**aya |
| **liqueur** | il liquore | lee**kwo**ray |
| **list** | la lista | **lee**sta |
| **to listen** (to) | ascoltare | askol-**ta**ray |
| **litre** | il litro | **lee**tro |
| **little** (small) | piccolo(a) | **peek**-kolo(a) |
| ***a little...*** | un po' di... | oon p**o** dee... |
| **to live** | vivere; abitare | **vee**vayray; abee**ta**ray |
| **local** | locale | lo**ka**lay |
| **to lock** | chiudere a chiave | kee**oo**dayray a kee**a**vay |
| **long** | lungo(a) | **loon**-go |
| ***for a long time*** | molto tempo | **mol**-to **tem**-po |

| | | |
|---|---|---|
| **to look after** | prendersi cura di | **pren**-dayrsee **koo**ra dee |
| **to look at** | guardare | goo-ar**da**ray |
| **to look for** | cercare | chayr-**ka**ray |
| **to lose** | perdere | **payr**dayray |
| **lost** (object) | perso(a) | **payr**so(a) |
| ***I've lost my...*** | ho perso il/la... | o **payr**so eel/la |
| ***I'm lost*** | mi sono smarrito(a) | mee **so**no zmar-**ree**to(a) |
| **lost property office** | l'ufficio oggetti smarriti *m* | oof-**fee**chyo od-**jayt**-tee zmar-**ree**tee |
| **lot:** ***a lot*** | molto | **mol**-to |
| **lounge** (in hotel) | il salone | sa**lo**nay |
| (in airport) | la sala d'attesa | **sa**la dat-**tay**za |
| **lovely** | bellissimo(a) | bel-**lees**-seemo(a) |
| **low** | basso(a) | **bas**-so(a) |
| (standard, quality) | scadente | ska**dayn**-tay |
| **to lower the volume** | abbassare il volume | ab-bas-**sa**ray eel vo**loo**may |
| **low-fat** | magro(a) | **ma**gro(a) |
| **lucky** | fortunato(a) | for-too**na**to(a) |
| **luggage** | i bagagli | ee ba**ga**lyee |
| **luggage trolley** | il carrello | kar-**rayl**-lo |
| **lunch** | il pranzo | **pran**-dzo |
| **luxury** | di lusso | dee **loos**-so |

## M

| | | |
|---|---|---|
| **magazine** | la rivista | reev**ee**sta |
| **maid** (in hotel) | la cameriera | kamayree**ay**ra |
| **mail** | la posta | **po**sta |
| **main** | principale | preenchee**pa**lay |
| **main course** (meal) | il secondo | say**kon**-do |
| **to make** | fare | **fa**ray |
| (meal) | preparare | praypa**ra**ray |
| **make-up** | il trucco | **trook**-ko |
| **man** | l'uomo *m* | oo-**o**mo |
| **manager** | il direttore | deerayt-**to**ray |
| **many** | molti(e) | **mol**-tee(ay) |
| **map** (of country) | la carta geografica | **kar**ta jay-o**gra**feeka |

| English | Italian | Pronunciation |
|---|---|---|
| (of city) | la piantina | peean**tee**na |
| **marmalade** | la marmellata d'arance | marmayl-**la**ta da**ran**che |
| **married** | sposato(a) | spo**za**to(a) |
| **marry**: ***to get married*** | sposarsi | spozar-see |
| **material** | il materiale | matay**reea**lay |
| **to matter** | importare | eem-por**ta**ray |
| ***it doesn't matter*** | non importa | non eem**por**ta |
| ***what's the matter?*** | cosa c'è? | **co**sa chay? |
| **maximum** | il massimo | **mas**-seemo |
| **me** | me; mi | may; mee |
| **meal** | il pasto | **pa**sto |
| **to mean** (signify) | voler dire | vo**layr dee**ray |
| ***what does it mean?*** | cosa vuol dire? | **co**sa vwol **dee**ray? |
| **meat** | la carne | **kar**-nay |
| **medicine** | la medicina | maydee**chee**na |
| **medium rare** (steak) | poco cotto(a) | **po**ko **kot**-to(a) |
| **to meet** | incontrare | eenkon-**tra**ray |
| ***pleased to meet you!*** | piacere! | peea**chay**ray! |
| **men** | gli uomini | oo-**o**meenee |
| **to mend** | riparare | reepa**ra**ray |
| **menu** | il menù | may**noo** |
| **message** | il messaggio | mays-**sad**-jo |
| **metre** | il metro | **may**tro |
| **metro** | la metropolitana | maytropolee**ta**na |
| **metro station** | la stazione del metrò | stat-**syo**nay dayl may**tro** |
| **midday** | il mezzogiorno | mayz-zod-**jor**no |
| ***at midday*** | a mezzogiorno | a mayz-zod-**jor**no |
| **middle** | il mezzo | **mayz**-zo |
| **middle-aged** | di mezz'età | dee medz-zay**ta** |
| **midnight** | la mezzanotte | medz-za**not**-tay |
| ***at midnight*** | a mezzanotte | a medz-za**not**-tay |
| **mild** | dolce; mite | **dol**-chay; **mee**tay |

# English - Italian



| English | Italian | Pronunciation |
|---|---|---|
| **milk** | il latte | **lat**-tay |
| **mind:** ***do you mind?*** | le dà fastidio? | lay da fas**tee**dyo? |
| ***I don't mind*** | non mi dà fastidio | non mee da fas**tee**dyo |
| **mineral water** | l'acqua minerale *f* | **ak**wa meenay**ra**lay |
| **minimum** | il minimo | **mee**neemo |
| **minute** | il minuto | mee**noo**to |
| **to miss** (train, etc) | perdere | **payr**dayray |
| **Miss** | Signorina | seenyo**ree**na |
| **missing** (thing) | smarrito(a) | zmar-**ree**to (a) |
| (person) | scomparso(a) | skom-**par**so |
| **mistake** | l'errore *m* | ayr-**ror**ay |
| **to mix** | mescolare | maysko**la**ray |
| **mobile phone** | il cellulare | chayl-loo**la**ray |
| **mobile number** | il numero di cellulare | **noo**mayro dee chayl-loo**la**ray |
| **modern** | moderno(a) | mo**dayr**-no |
| **moment:** ***just a moment*** | un momento | oon mo**mayn**to |
| **money** | i soldi | ee **sol**-dee |
| **month** | il mese | **may**say |
| ***this month*** | questo mese | **kway**sto **may**say |
| ***last month*** | il mese scorso | **may**say **skor**-so |
| ***next month*** | il mese prossimo | **may**say **pros**-seemo |
| **more** (than) | più (di) | py**oo** (dee) |
| **morning** | la mattina | mat-**tee**na |
| ***in the morning*** | di mattina | dee mat-**tee**na |
| ***this morning*** | stamattina | stamat-**tee**na |
| ***tomorrow morning*** | domani mattina | do-**ma**nee mat-**tee**na |
| **most** | il/la più; il massimo | py**oo**; **mas**-seemo |
| **mother** | la madre | **ma**dray |
| **motor** | il motore | mo**to**ray |
| **motorbike** | la moto | **mo**to |
| **motorway** | l'autostrada *f* | aooto**stra**da |
| **mouth** | la bocca | **bok**-ka |
| **move** | muoversi | **mwo**-vayrsee |

| | | |
|---|---|---|
| **movie** | il film | feelm |
| **Mr** | Signor | see**nyor** |
| **Mrs** | Signora | see**nyo**ra |
| **Ms** | Signora | see**nyo**ra |
| **much** | molto | **mol**-to |
| ***too much*** | troppo | **trop**-po |
| **mugging** | lo scippo | **sheep**-po |
| **muscle** | il muscolo | **moos**-kolo |
| **museum** | il museo | moo**zay**-o |
| **music** | la musica | **moo**zeeka |
| **must** (to have to) | dovere | do**vay**ray |
| ***I must*** | devo | **day**vo |
| ***I mustn't*** | non devo | non **day**vo |
| **my** | il/la mio(a) | m**ee**o (a) |

## N

| | | |
|---|---|---|
| **name** | il nome | **no**may |
| **narrow** | stretto(a) | **strayt**-to(a) |
| **nationality** | la nazionalità | natseeonalee**ta** |
| **nature** | la natura | na**too**ra |
| **near to** | vicino(a) a | vee**chee**no(a) a |
| **necessary** | necessario(a) | nayches-**sa**reeo(a) |
| **to need** | avere bisogno di... | a**vay**ray bee**zo**nyo dee... |
| ***I need...*** | ho bisogno di... | o bee**zo**nyo dee... |
| **never** | mai | m**a**ee |
| **new** | nuovo(a) | **nwo**-vo(a) |
| **news** (on television) | le notizie | no**tee**tseeay |
| | il telegiornale | taylaydjor**na**lay |
| **newspaper** | il giornale | djor**na**lay |
| **New Year** | il Capodanno | kapo**dan**-no |
| **next** | prossimo(a) | **pros**-seemo(a) |
| ***next to*** | accanto a | ak-**kan**-to a |
| ***next week*** | la settimana prossima | sayt-tee**ma**na **pros**-seema |
| **nice** (person) | piacevole | pya-**chay**volay |
| | simpatico(a) | seem-**pa**teeko(a) |
| **night** | la notte | **not**-tay |
| ***at night*** | di notte | dee **not**-tay |
| ***last night*** | ieri sera | ee**ay**ree **say**-ra |
| ***tonight*** | stasera | sta**sayra** |

| | | |
|---|---|---|
| **no** | no | no |
| ***no entry*** | vietato l'ingresso | veeay**ta**to leen**gres**-so |
| ***no smoking*** | vietato fumare | veeay**ta**to foo**ma**ray |
| (without) | senza | **sayn**tsa |
| **nobody** | nessuno | nays-**soo**no |
| **noise** | il rumore | roo**mo**ray |
| **noisy** | rumoroso(a) | roomo**ro**so(a) |
| **non-alcoholic** | analcolico(a) | anal-**ko**leeko |
| **no-one** | nessuno(a) | nays-**soo**no(a) |
| **north** | il nord | nord |
| **nose** | il naso | **na**-so |
| **not** | non | non |
| ***I do not know*** | non lo so | non lo so |
| **nothing** | niente | nee**ayn**tay |
| ***nothing else*** | nient'altro | neeayn**tal**-tro |
| **notice** | l'avviso *m* | av-**vee**zo |
| **now** | adesso | a**days**-so |
| **nowhere** | da nessuna parte | da nays-**soo**na **par**-tay |
| **number** | il numero | **noo**mayro |

## O

| | | |
|---|---|---|
| **of** | di | dee |
| ***a glass of water*** | un bicchiere d'acqua | oon beek-**kyay**ray **da**kwa |
| ***made of...*** | fatto di... | **fat**-to dee... |
| **off** (machine, etc) | spento(a) | **spayn**-to(a) |
| (milk, food) | andato(a) a male | an**da**to(a) a **ma**lay |
| **office** | l'ufficio *m* | oof-**fee**chyo |
| **often** | spesso | **spays**-so |
| ***how often?*** | ogni quanto? | **o**nyee **kwan**to? |
| **OK!** | va bene! | va **be**nay! |
| **old** | vecchio(a) | **vayk**-kyo(a) |
| **on** (light, engine) | acceso(a) | a-**chay**so(a) |
| (tap) | aperto(a) | a-**payr**to(a) |
| **once** | una volta | **oo**na **vol**-ta |
| ***at once*** | subito | **soo**-beeto |
| **only** | solo | **so**lo |

| | | |
|---|---|---|
| **open** | aperto(a) | a-**payr**to(a) |
| **to open** | aprire | a-**pree**ray |
| **opposite** | di fronte a | dee **fron**-tay a |
| **or** | o | o |
| **orange** (colour) | arancione | aran**chyo**nay |
| **orange** (fruit) | l'arancia *f* | a**ran**chya |
| **orange juice** | il succo d'arancia | **sook**-ko da**ran**chya |
| **order** | l'ordine *m* | **o**rdeenay |
| ***out of order*** | fuori servizio | **fwor**ee sayr**vee**tsyo |
| **to order** (food) | ordinare | ordee**na**ray |
| **organic** | biologico(a) | byo**lo**jeeko(a) |
| **to organize** | organizzare | organeed-**za**ray |
| **other** | l'altro(a) | **al**-tro(a) |
| **our** | il/la nostro(a) | **nos**tro(a) |
| **out** (light) | spento(a) | **spayn**-to(a) |
| **over** (on top of) | sopra | **so**pra |
| **to overbook** | accettare troppe prenotazioni | ac-chayt-**ta**ray **trop**-pay praynota**tsyo**nee |
| **to overcharge** | far pagare troppo | far pa**ga**ray **trop**-po |
| **overdone** (food) | troppo cotto(a) | **trop**-po **kot**-to(a) |
| **to owe** | dovere | do**vay**ray |
| ***I owe you...*** | le devo... | lay **dey**vo... |
| ***you owe me...*** | mi deve... | mee **day**vay... |

## P

| | | |
|---|---|---|
| **package** | il pacco | **pak**-ko |
| **package tour** | il viaggio organizzato | **vyad**-jo organeed-**za**to |
| **paid** | pagato(a) | pa**ga**to(a) |
| ***I've paid*** | ho pagato | o pa**ga**to |
| **pain** | il dolore | do**lo**ray |
| **painful** | doloroso(a) | dolo**ro**so(a) |
| **painting** (picture) | il quadro | **kwa**dro |
| **pair** | il paio | **pa**yo |
| **palace** | il palazzo | pa**lat**-so |
| **pale** | pallido(a) | **pal**-leedo(a) |
| **pants** | le mutande | moo**tan**-day |
| **paper** | la carta | **kar**-ta |

| English | Italian | Pronunciation |
|---|---|---|
| **parcel** | il pacco | **pak**-ko |
| **pardon?** | scusi? | **skoo**zee? |
| ***I beg your pardon*** | mi scusi | mee **skoo**zee |
| **parents** | i genitori | jaynee**to**ree |
| **park** | il parco | **par**-ko |
| **to park** | parcheggiare | parkayd-**ja**ray |
| **parmesan** | il parmigiano | parmee-**ja**no |
| **partner** (business) | il/la socio(a) | **so**chyo(a) |
| (boy/girlfriend) | il/la compagno(a) | kom**pa**nyo(a) |
| **party** (celebration) | la festa | **fay**sta |
| **passenger** | il/la passeggero(a) | pas-sayd-**jay**ro(a) |
| **passport** | il passaporto | pas-sa**por**to |
| **pastry** | la pasta | **pas**-ta |
| **to pay** | pagare | pa**ga**ray |
| ***payment*** | il pagamento | paga**mayn**-to |
| **peaches** | le pesche | **pays**-kay |
| **peanut allergy** | l'allergia alle arachidi *f* | al-layr-**djee**a allay a**ra**keedee |
| **pears** | le pere | **pay**ray |
| **peas** | i piselli | pee**sayl**-lee |
| **pen** | la penna | **payn**-na |
| **pensioner** | il/la pensionato(a) | pen-syo**na**to(a) |
| **people** | la gente | **jen**-tay |
| **pepper** (spice) | il pepe | **pay**pay |
| (vegetable) | il peperone | paypay**ro**nay |
| **per:** ***per day*** | al giorno | al **jor**-no |
| ***per week*** | alla settimana | alla set-tee-**ma**na |
| ***per person*** | a persona | a payr**so**na |
| **performance** | la rappresentazione | rap-praysayn-tat**syo**nay |
| **perhaps** | forse | **for**say |
| **person** | la persona | payr-**so**na |
| **petrol** | la benzina | ben**zee**na |
| **petrol station** | la stazione di servizio | stat-**syo**nay dee sayr-**veet**- syo |
| **pharmacy** | la farmacia | far-ma**chya** |

| English | Italian | Pronunciation |
|---|---|---|
| **to photocopy** | fotocopiare | fotoko**pya**ray |
| **photograph** | la foto | **fo**to |
| ***to take a photo*** | fare una foto | **fa**ray oona **fo**to |
| **piece** | il pezzo | **payt**-so |
| **pillow** | il cuscino | koo**shee**no |
| **pink** | rosa | **ro**za |
| **pity**: ***what a pity!*** | che peccato! | kay payk-**ka**to! |
| **place** | il luogo | **lwo**go |
| ***place of birth*** | il luogo di nascita | **lwo**go dee **na**sheeta |
| **plan** | il piano | **pya**no |
| **to plan** | progettare | projet-**ta**ray |
| **plane** | l'aereo *m* | a-**ay**-ray-o |
| **plastic** (made of) | di plastica | dee **plas**-teeka |
| **platform** (railway) | il binario | bee**na**ryo |
| ***from which platform?*** | da quale binario? | da **kwa**lay bee**na**ryo? |
| **play** (theatre) | la commedia | kom-**may**dya |
| **to play** (games) | giocare | jo**ka**ray |
| **please** | per favore; prego | payr fa**vo**ray; **pray**go |
| **pleased to meet you** | piacere | pya**chay**ray |
| **plum** | la prugna | **proo**-nya |
| **p.m.** | del pomeriggio | dayl pomay-**ree**-djo |
| **poached** (egg) | in camicia | een ka**mee**chya |
| (fish) | bollito(a) | bol-**lee**to(a) |
| **point** | il punto | **poon**-to |
| **poisonous** | velenoso(a) | vaylay**no**zo(a) |
| **police** | la polizia | polee**tzee**-ya |
| **police station** | il commissariato | kom-mees-sa**rya**to |
| **pool** (swimming) | la piscina | pee**shee**na |
| **poor** | povero(a) | **po**vayro(a) |
| **pope** | il papa | **pa**pa |
| **pork** | la carne di maiale | **kar**nay dee ma**ya**lay |

| English | Italian | Pronunciation |
|---|---|---|
| **porter** (for luggage) | il portiere | por**teeay**-ray |
| | il facchino | fak-**kee**no |
| **possible** | possibile | pos-**see**beelay |
| **post:** ***by post*** | per posta | payr **pos**-ta |
| **to post** (letters) | imbucare | eembоo**ka**ray |
| **postbox** | la buca delle lettere | **boo**ka daylay **let**-tayray |
| **postcard** | la cartolina | karto**leena** |
| **postcode** | il codice postale | **ko**deechay pos-**ta**lay |
| **post office** | l'ufficio postale *m* | oof-**fee**chyo pos-**ta**lay |
| **to postpone** | rimandare | reeman**da**ray |
| **potato** | la patata | pa**ta**ta |
| **pound** (money) | la sterlina | stayr**lee**na |
| **to pour** | versare | vayr**sa**ray |
| **power** (electricity) | l'elettricità | elet-treechee**ta** |
| **to prefer** | preferire | prayfay**ree**ray |
| **to prepare** | preparare | praypa**ra**ray |
| **prescription** | la ricetta | ree**chayt**-ta |

| English | Italian | Pronunciation |
|---|---|---|
| **present** (gift) | il regalo | ray**ga**lo |
| **pretty** | carino(a) | ka**ree**no(a) |
| **price** | il prezzo | **prayt**-so |
| **price list** | il listino prezzi | lees-**tee**no **prayt**-see |
| **private** | privato(a) | pree**va**to(a) |
| **probably** | probabilmente | probabeel-**mayn**tay |
| **problem** | il problema | pro**blay**ma |
| **prohibited** | proibito(a) | pro-ee**bee**to(a) |
| **promise** | la promessa | pro**mays**sa |
| **to promise** | promettere | pro**mayt**-tayray |
| **to pronounce** | pronunciare | pronoon**chya**ray |
| ***how's it pronounced?*** | come si pronuncia? | **ko**may see pro**noon**chya? |
| **public** | pubblico(a) | poob-**blee**ko(a) |
| **public holiday** | la festa nazionale | **fays**-ta nat-syo**na**lay |
| **pudding** | il dessert | days-**sayrt** |
| **to pull** | tirare | tee**ra**ray |

**purple** viola **vyo**la
**purse** il borsellino bor-sayl-**lee**no
**to push** spingere **speen**-jayray
**to put** (to place) mettere **mayt**-tayray
**pyjamas** il pigiama pee**ja**ma

## Q

**quality** la qualità kwalee**ta**
**quantity** la quantità kwantee**ta**
**to quarrel** litigare leetee**ga**ray
**quarter:**
*a quarter* un quarto oon **kwar**-to
**question** la domanda do**man**-da
**queue** la coda **ko**da
**to queue** fare la coda **fa**ray la **ko**da
**quick** veloce vay**lo**chay
**quickly** velocemente vaylochay-**mayn**tay
**quiet** (place) tranquillo(a) trankw**eel**-lo(a)
**quite** (rather) piuttosto pyoot-**to**sto

## R

**race** (sport) la gara **ga**ra
**racket** (tennis) la racchetta rak-**ket**-ta
**radio** la radio **ra**dyo
**railway station** la stazione dei treni stat**syo**-nay dey **tray**nee
**rain** la pioggia **pyo**-dja
**to rain** piovere **pyo**vayray
**raincoat** l'impermeabile *m* eempermay-**a**-beelay
**raped** violentata vyolayn**ta**ta
**rare** (unique) (steak) raro(a) **ra**ro(a) al sangue al **san**-gway
**raspberries** i lamponi lam**po**nee
**rate** (cost) la tariffa ta**reef**-fa
**rate of exchange** il cambio **kam**-byo
**raw** crudo(a) **kroo**do(a)
**razor** il rasoio ra**zo**yo
**razor blades** le lamette la**mayt**-tay
**to read** leggere **layd**-jayray

# English - Italian

| English | Italian | Pronunciation |
|---|---|---|
| **ready** | pronto(a) | **pron**-to(a) |
| ***to get ready*** | prepararsi | prayp**arar**-see |
| **real** | vero(a) | **vay**ro(a) |
| **to realize** | rendersi conto di | rayn**der**-see **kon**-to dee |
| **receipt** | la ricevuta | reechay**voo**ta |
| **reception** (desk) | la reception | ray**sayp**-shyon |
| **receptionist** | l'addetto(a) | ad-**dayt**-to(a) |
| **to recognize** | riconoscere | reeko**no**shayray |
| **to recommend** | raccomandare | rak-koman**da**ray |
| **red** | rosso(a) | **ros**-so(a) |
| **to reduce** | ridurre | ree**door**-ray |
| **reduction** | la riduzione | reedoot-**syo**nay |
| **refund** | il rimborso | reem**bor**-so |
| **to refuse** | rifiutare | reefyoo**ta**ray |
| **region** | la regione | re**jo**nay |
| **register** | il registro | ray**jees**-tro |
| **registration form** | il modulo d'iscrizione | **mo**doolo dees-cree-**tsyo**nay |
| **to reimburse** | rimborsare | reem-bor**sa**ray |
| **relation** (family) | il/la parente | pa**rayn**tay |
| **relationship** | il rapporto | rap-**por**-to |
| **to remember** | ricordare | reekor**da**ray |
| ***I don't remember*** | non mi ricordo | non mee ree**kor**-do |
| **to remove** | togliere | to**lye**ray |
| **repair** | la riparazione | reepara**tsyo**nay |
| **to repair** | riparare | reepa**ra**ray |
| **to repeat** | ripetere | ree**pay**tayray |
| **to reply** | rispondere | rees**pon**dayray |
| **to report** (crime) | denunciare | daynoon**chya**ray |
| **request** | la richiesta | ree**kye**sta |
| **to request** | richiedere | ree**kye**dayray |
| **reservation** | la prenotazione | praynota**tsyo**nay |
| **to reserve** | prenotare | prayno**ta**ray |
| **reserved** | prenotato(a) | prayno**ta**to(a) |
| **rest** (repose) | il riposo | ree**po**so |
| (remainder) | il resto | res-**to** |
| **to rest** | riposarsi | reepo**sar**see |
| **restaurant** | il ristorante | reesto**ran**tay |

| English | Italian | Pronunciation |
|---|---|---|
| **restaurant car** | il vagone ristorante | va**go**nay reesto**ran**tay |
| **retired:** | | |
| ***I'm retired*** | sono in pensione | **so**no een pen**syo**nay |
| **to return** (go back) | ritornare | reetor**na**ray |
| (to give back) | restituire | res-tee-**twee**ray |
| **return ticket** | il biglietto di andata e ritorno | eel bee**lye**t-to dee an**da**ta ay ree**to**rno |
| **rice** | il riso | **ree**zo |
| **rich** | ricco(a) | **reek**-ko(a) |
| **right** (correct) | giusto(a) | **joos**-to(a) |
| **right** (not left) | la destra | **des**tra |
| ***at/to the right*** | a destra | a **des**tra |
| **to ring** (bell) | suonare | swo**na**ray |
| (phone) | squillare | sqweel-**la**ray |
| **ring** | l'anello *m* | a**nayl**lo |
| **ring road** | la circonvallazione | cheerkon-val-la**tsyo**nay |
| **road** | la strada | **stra**-da |
| **road map** | la carta stradale | **kar**-ta stra-**da**-lay |
| **road sign** | il cartello stradale | kar-**tayl**-lo stra-**da**-lay |
| **roast** | arrosto(a) | ar-**ro**sto |
| **roll** (bread) | il panino | pa**nee**no |
| **room** (hotel) | la camera | **ka**mayra |
| ***double room*** | la camera doppia | **ka**mayra **dop**-pya |
| ***family room*** | la camera per famiglia | **ka**mayra payr fa**mee**lya |
| ***single room*** | la camera singola | **ka**mayra **seen**gola |
| **room number** | il numero di camera | **noo**mayro dee **ka**mayra |
| **room service** | il servizio in camera | ser**vee**tsyo een **ka**mayra |
| **round** | rotondo(a) | ro-**ton**-do(a) |
| **row** (in theatre) | la fila | **fee**la |
| **to run** | correre | **kor**-rayray |

## S

| English | Italian | Pronunciation |
|---|---|---|
| **safe** (for valuables) | la cassaforte | kas-sa-**fort**ay |
| **safe** (medicine, etc) | senza pericolo; sicuro(a) | **sen**tsa pe-**reek**olo; see-**koor**o(a) |
| ***is it safe?*** | è senza pericolo? | e **sen**tsa pe-**reek**olo? |
| **safety** | la sicurezza | seekoo-**rets**-sa |
| **salad** | l'insalata *f* | eensa-**lat**a |
| ***green/mixed salad*** | l'insalata verde/ mista | eensa-**lat**a **vayr**day/ **mees**ta |
| **salami** | il salame | sa-**lam**ay |
| **sales** (reductions) | i saldi | **sal**dee |
| **salesman/ woman** | il/la commesso(a) | kom-**mes**-so(a) |
| **salt** | il sale | **sal**ay |
| **salty** | salato(a) | sa-**lat**o(a) |
| **same** | stesso(a) | **stes**-so(a) |
| **sand** | la sabbia | **sab**-bya |
| **sandwich** | il panino; il tramezzino | pa-**nee**no; tra-med-**zee**no |
| ***toasted sandwich*** | il toast | tost |
| **satellite TV** | la televisione via satellite | televeez-**yon**ay **vee**-a sa-**tel**-leetay |
| **sauce** | la salsa | **sal**sa |
| **savoury** (not sweet) | salato(a) | sa-**lat**o(a) |
| **to say** | dire | **deer**ay |
| **scarf** | la sciarpa | **sharp**a |
| (headscarf) | il foulard | foo-**lar** |
| **school** | la scuola | **skwol**a |
| **sculpture** | la scultura | skool-**toor**a |
| **sea** | il mare | **mar**ay |
| **seafood** | i frutti di mare | **froot**-tee dee **mar**ay |
| **to search** | cercare | cher-**kar**ay |
| **seaside**: ***at the seaside*** | al mare | al **mar**ay |

| English | Italian | Pronunciation |
|---|---|---|
| **season** (of year) | la stagione | stad-**jon**ay |
| **seasoning** | il condimento | kondee-**men**to |
| **season ticket** | l'abbonamento | ab-bona-**men**to |
| **seat** (chair) | la sedia | **sed**-ya |
| (theatre, plane) | il posto | **pos**to |
| **seatbelt** | la cintura di sicurezza | cheen-**toor**a dee seekoo-**rets**-sa |
| **second** (time) | il secondo | se-**kon**do |
| **second** | secondo(a) | se-**kon**do(a) |
| ***second class*** | la seconda classe | se-**kon**da **klas**-say |
| **to see** | vedere | ve-**day**ray |
| **to sell** | vendere | **ven**-deray |
| ***do you sell...?*** | vende...? | **ven**day? |
| **sell-by date** | la data di scadenza | **da**ta dee ska-**den**tsa |
| **to send** | mandare; spedire | man-**dar**ay; spe-**dee**ray |
| **service charge** | il servizio | ser-**veets**-yo |
| **service station** | la stazione di servizio | stats-**yon**ay dee ser-**veets**-yo |

| English | Italian | Pronunciation |
|---|---|---|
| **set menu** | il menù turistico/ fisso | may-**noo** too-**rees**-teeko/**fees**-so |
| **several** | alcuni(e) | al-**koon**ee(ay) |
| **sex** (gender) | il sesso | **ses**-so |
| (intercourse) | i rapporti sessuali | rap-**por**tee ses-soo-**al**ee |
| **shade** | l'ombra *f* | **om**bra |
| **shampoo** | lo shampoo | **sham**poo |
| **to share** | dividere | dee-**vee**dayray |
| **sharp** (blade) | affilato(a) | af-fee-**lat**o(a) |
| **to shave** | farsi la barba | **far**see la **bar**ba |
| **shaver** | il rasoio | ra-**soy**o |
| **she** | lei | lay |
| **sheet** (bed) | il lenzuolo | len-**zwo**lo |
| **shellfish** | i frutti di mare | **froot**-tee dee **mar**ay |
| **sheltered** | riparato(a) | reepa-**rat**o(a) |
| **to shine** | brillare | bril-**lar**ay |
| **shirt** | la camicia | ka-**meech**a |
| **shoe** | la scarpa | **skar**pa |

| English | Italian | Pronunciation |
|---|---|---|
| **shop** | il negozio | ne-**gots**-yo |
| **to shop** | fare la spesa | **fa**ray la **spes**a |
| **shop assistant** | il/la commesso(a) | kom-**mes**-so(a) |
| **short** (person) | corto(a) basso(a) | **kor**to(a) **bas**-so(a) |
| **shorts** | i calzoncini corti | kaltson-**chee**nee **kor**tee |
| **shoulder** | la spalla | **spal**-la |
| **show** (theatre) | lo spettacolo | spet-**ta**-kolo |
| **to show** | mostrare | mos-**trar**ay |
| **shower** | la doccia | **dot**-cha |
| (rain) | il rovescio | ro-**vesh**o |
| **to shrink** | restringersi | res-**trin**-jersee |
| **shut** (closed) | chiuso(a) | **kyoo**zo(a) |
| **sick** (ill) | malato(a) | ma-**lat**o(a) |
| **side** | il lato | **lat**o |
| **sightseeing tour** | il giro turistico | **jeer**o too-**rees**teeko |
| **sign** | il segno | **sen**-yo |
| (on road) | il segnale | sen-**yal**ay |

| English | Italian | Pronunciation |
|---|---|---|
| **to sign** | firmare | feer-**mar**ay |
| **signature** | la firma | **feer**ma |
| **silk** | la seta | **se**ta |
| **silver** | l'argento *m* | ar-**jent**o |
| **similar to** | simile a | **seem**-eelay a |
| **since** (time) | da | da |
| **to sing** | cantare | kan-**tar**ay |
| **single** (unmarried) | non sposato(a) | non spo-**zat**o(a) |
| (not double) | singolo(a) | **seen**-golo(a) |
| (ticket) | di (sola) andata | dee (**so**la) an-**da**ta |
| ***single bed*** | il letto a una piazza | **let**-to a oona **pee**-at-tsa |
| ***single room*** | la camera singola | **ka**-mayra **seen**-gola |
| **sir** | signore | seen-**yor**ay |
| **sister** | la sorella | so-**rel**-la |
| **to sit** | sedersi | se-**dayr**-see |
| ***please, sit down*** | prego, si accomodi | ak-**pray**go, see **kom**odee |

| | | |
|---|---|---|
| **size** (of clothes) | la taglia | **tal**-ya |
| (of shoes) | il numero | **noo**-mayro |
| **to ski** | sciare | shee-**ar**ay |
| **skis** | gli sci | shee |
| **ski instructor** | il/la maestro(a) di sci | ma-**ay**stro(a) dee shee |
| **skin** | la pelle | **pel**-lay |
| **skirt** | la gonna | **gon**-na |
| **sky** | il cielo | **chel**o |
| **to sleep** | dormire | dor-**meer**ay |
| ***to sleep in*** | dormire fino a tardi | dor-**meer**ay **fee**no a **tar**dee |
| **slice** (piece of) | la fetta | **fet**-ta |
| **slide** (photo) | la diapositiva | deea-pozee-**teev**a |
| **slow** | lento(a) | **len**to(a) |
| **to slow down** | rallentare | ral-len-**tar**ay |
| **slowly** | lentamente | lenta-**men**tay |
| **small** | piccolo(a) | **peek**-kolo(a) |
| **smell** | l'odore *m* | o-**dor**ay |
| **to smell** (bad) | puzzare | poot-**tsar**ay |
| **smile** | il sorriso | sor-**rees**o |
| **to smile** | sorridere | sor-**reed**-eray |
| **smoke** | il fumo | **foom**o |
| **to smoke** | fumare | foo-**mar**ay |
| ***I don't smoke*** | non fumo | non **foom**o |
| ***can I smoke?*** | posso fumare? | **pos**-so foo-**mar**ay? |
| **snack** | lo spuntino | spoon-**teen**o |
| **to sneeze** | starnutire | starnoo-**teer**ay |
| **snow** | la neve | **nev**ay |
| **to snow:** *it's snowing* | nevica | **nay**-veeka |
| **soap** | il sapone | sa-**pon**ay |
| **sofa** | il divano | dee-**van**o |
| **soft** | soffice; morbido(a) | **sof**-feechay; **mor**-beedo(a) |
| **soft drink** | la bibita | **bee**-beeta |
| **some** | di (del/della) | dee (del/**del**-la) |
| (a few) | alcuni/alcune | al-**koon**ee/ al-**koon**ay |
| **someone** | qualcuno | kwal-**koon**o |

| English | Italian | Pronunciation |
|---|---|---|
| **something** | qualcosa | kwal-**ko**za |
| **sometimes** | qualche volta | **kwal**kay **vol**ta |
| **son** | il figlio | **feel**-yo |
| **song** | la canzone | kan-**tson**ay |
| **soon** | presto | **pres**to |
| ***as soon as possible*** | il più presto possibile | pyoo **pres**to pos-**see**-beelay |
| **sore throat** | il mal di gola | mal dee **go**la |
| **sorry:** ***I'm sorry!*** | mi scusi! | mee **skoo**zee! |
| **soup** | la minestra | mee-**nes**-tra |
| **sour** | aspro(a); agro(a) | **asp**ro(a); **ag**ro(a) |
| **south** | il sud | sood |
| **souvenir** | il souvenir | soovay-**neer** |
| **space** | lo spazio | **spats**-yo |
| (parking) | il posteggio | pos-**ted**-jo |
| **sparkling** | frizzante | freed-**zan**tay |
| **to speak** | parlare | par-**lar**ay |
| ***do you speak English?*** | parla inglese? | **par**la een-**glay**say? |
| **speciality** | la specialità | spetcha-lee-**ta** |
| **speed** | la velocità | velo-chee-**ta** |
| **speed limit** | il limite di velocità | **lee**-meetay dee velo-chee-**ta** |
| **speeding** | l'eccesso di velocità *m* | et-**ches**-so dee velo-chee-**ta** |
| **to spell** | scrivere | **skreev**-eray |
| ***how's it spelt?*** | come si scrive? | **kom**ay see **skree**vay? |
| **to spend** | spendere | **spen**-deray |
| **spice** | le spezie | **spets**-yay |
| **spicy** | piccante | peek-**kan**tay |
| **spinach** | gli spinaci | spee-**nach**ee |
| **spirits** (alcohol) | i liquori | lee-**kwor**ee |
| **spoon** | il cucchiaio | kook-**kya**-yo |
| **sport** | lo sport | sport |
| **spot** (stain) | la macchia | **mak**-kya |
| (place) | il posto | **pos**to |
| **spring** (season) | la primavera | preema-**ver**a |
| **square** (in town) | la piazza | **pee**-at-tsa |
| **to squeeze** | spremere; stringere | **sprem**-eray; **strin**-jeray |
| **stadium** | lo stadio | **stad**-yo |

| English | Italian | Pronunciation |
|---|---|---|
| **staff** | il personale | perso-**nal**ay |
| **stain** | la macchia | **mak**-kya |
| **stairs** | le scale | **ska**lay |
| **stamp** | il francobollo | franko-**bol**-lo |
| **to stand** | stare in piedi | **sta**ray een **pyed**ee |
| **star** | la stella | **stel**-la |
| **start** | l'inizio *m* | ee-**neets**-yo |
| **to start** | cominciare | komeen-**char**ay |
| **starter** (food) | l'antipasto *m* | antee-**pas**to |
| **station** | la stazione | stats-**yon**ay |
| **statue** | la statua | **stat**-ooa |
| **stay** | il soggiorno | sod-**jorn**o |
| ***to stay*** (remain) | rimanere | reema-**nayr**ay |
| ***I'm staying at the Grand Hotel*** | sono al Grand Hotel | **son**o al gran-do-**tel** |
| **steak** | la bistecca | bees-**tek**-ka |
| **to steal** | rubare | roo-**bar**ay |
| **steep:** ***is it steep?*** | è in salita? | e een sa-**lee**ta? |
| **step** (stair) | il gradino | gra-**dee**no |
| **sterling** | la sterlina | stayr-**leen**a |
| **to stick** (with glue) | incollare | eenkol-**lar**ay |
| **still** (motionless) | fermo(a) | **fayr**mo(a) |
| (water) | naturale | natoo-**ral**ay |
| (yet) | ancora | an-**kor**a |
| **stolen** | rubato(a) | roo-**bat**o(a) |
| **stomach** | lo stomaco | **sto**-mako |
| **stomach ache** | il mal di stomaco | mal dee **sto**-mako |
| **stone** | la pietra | **pyet**-tra |
| **to stop** (halt) | fermarsi | fayr-**mar**see |
| (stop doing) | smettere | **zmayt**-tayray |
| **storey** | il piano | **pyan**o |
| **storm** | la tempesta; il temporale | tem-**pest**a; tempo-**ral**ay |
| **straight away** | subito | **soo**-beeto |
| **straight on** | diritto | dee-**reet**-to |
| **strange** | strano(a) | **stra**no(a) |
| **straw** (drinking) | la cannuccia | kan-**noot**-cha |
| **strawberries** | le fragole | **fra**-golay |
| **street map** | la piantina | peean-**teen**a |

| English | Italian | Pronunciation |
|---|---|---|
| **stroke** (medical) | l'ictus *m* | **eek**-toos |
| **strong** | forte | **for**tay |
| **student** | lo studente/ la studentessa | stoo-**den**tay/ stooden-**tes**-sa |
| **student discount** | lo sconto per studenti | **skon**to payr stoo-**den**tee |
| **stung** | punto(a) | **poon**to(a) |
| **stupid** | stupido(a) | **stoo**-peedo(a) |
| **suddenly** | all'improvviso | al-leemprov-**veez**o |
| **suede** | la pelle scamosciata | **pel**-lay skamo-**sha**ta |
| **sugar** | lo zucchero | **tsook**-kayro |
| **sugar-free** | senza zucchero | **sen**tsa **tsook**-kayro |
| **suit** (man's) | l'abito *m* | **a**-beeto |
| (woman's) | il tailleur | ta-**yer** |
| **suitcase** | la valigia | va-**lee**ja |
| **summer** | l'estate *f* | es-**tat**ay |
| **sun** | il sole | **sol**ay |
| **to sunbathe** | prendere il sole | **pren**-deray eel **sol**ay |
| **sunblock** | la protezione solare totale | pro-tets-**yon**ay so-**lar**ay to-**tal**ay |
| **sunburn** | la scottatura solare | skot-ta-**toor**a so-**lar**ay |
| **suncream** | la crema solare | **krem**a so-**la**ray |
| **sunglasses** | gli occhiali da sole | ok-**yal**ee da **sol**ay |
| **sunny:** ***it's sunny*** | c'è il sole | che eel **sol**ay |
| **sunstroke** | l'insolazione *f* | eensolats-**yon**ay |
| **supermarket** | il supermercato | soopayr-mayr-**kat**o |
| **supper** (dinner) | la cena | **chay**na |
| **supplement** | il supplemento | soop-play-**ment**o |
| **sure:** ***I'm sure*** | sono sicuro(a) | **so**no see-**koor**o(a) |
| **surname** | il cognome | kon-**yom**ay |
| ***my surname is...*** | di cognome mi chiamo... | dee kon-**yom**ay mee **kya**-mo... |

**surprise** la sorpresa sor-**prays**a
**sweet** (not savoury) dolce **dol**chay
**sweetener** il dolcificante dolcheefee-**kant**ay
**sweets** le caramelle kara-**mel**-lay
**to swim** nuotare nwo-**tar**ay
**swimming pool** la piscina pee-**sheen**a
**swimsuit** il costume da bagno kos-**toom**ay da **ban**-yo
**to switch off** spegnere **spen**-yeray
**to switch on** accendere at-**chen**-deray
**swollen** gonfio(a) **gonf**-yo(a)

## T

**table** la tavola **tav**ola
**tablet** (pill) la pastiglia pas-**teel**-ya
**table tennis** il ping pong peeng-**pong**
**table wine** il vino da tavola **vee**no da **tav**ola
**to take** (carry) portare por-**tar**ay
(to grab, seize) prendere **pren**-deray
***how long does it take?*** quanto tempo ci vuole? **kwan**to **tem**po chee **vwol**ay?
**takeaway** (food) da asporto da-as-**por**to
**to take off** (plane) decollare dekol-**lar**ay
**to talk** parlare par-**lar**ay
**tall** alto(a) **al**to(a)
**tangerine** il mandarino manda-**reen**o
**tart** la crostata kros-**tat**a
**taste** il sapore sa-**por**ay
**to taste** assaggiare as-sad-**jar**ay
***can I taste some?*** ne posso assaggiare un po'? nay **pos**-so as-sad-**jar**ay oon po?
**tax** la tassa **tas**-sa
**taxi** il taxi **tak**see
**tea** il tè tay
***herbal tea*** la tisana tee-**zan**a
**teacher** l'insegnante (*m/f*) eensen-**yant**ay
**teaspoon** il cucchiaino kook-kya-**een**o
**telephone** il telefono te-**lef**ono

| English | Italian | Pronunciation |
|---|---|---|
| ***by telephone*** | per telefono | payr tay**lay**fono |
| **to telephone** | telefonare | telefo-**nar**ay |
| **telephone box** | la cabina telefonica | ka-**been**a tele-**fon**eeka |
| **telephone call** | la telefonata | telefo-**nat**a |
| **telephone card** | la scheda telefonica | **skay**da tele-**fon**eeka |
| **telephone number** | il numero di telefono | **noo**-mayro dee te-**lef**ono |
| **television** | la televisione | televeez-**yon**ay |
| **to tell** | dire | **deer**ay |
| **temperature** | la temperatura | tempayra-**toor**a |
| ***to have a (high) temperature*** | avere la febbre | a-**vay**ray la **feb**-bray |
| **temporary** | provvisorio(a) | prov-vee-**zor**-yo(a) |
| **tennis** | il tennis | **ten**-nees |
| **to test** (try out) | provare | pro-**var**ay |
| **to thank** | ringraziare | reengrats-**yar**ay |
| **thank you (very much)** | (molte) grazie | (**mol**tay) **grats**-yay |
| **that** | quel/quella/quello | kwel/**kwel**-la/**kwel**-lo |
| ***that one*** | quello(a) là | **kwel**-lo(a) la |
| **the** (sing) | il/lo/la | eel/lo/la |
| (plural) | i/gli/le | ee/lyee/lay |
| **theatre** | il teatro | tay-**at**ro |
| **theft** | il furto | **foor**to |
| **their** | il/la loro | **lor**o |
| **them, they** | loro; li; le | **lor**o; lee; lay |
| **there** (over there) | lì/là | lee/la |
| **there is/are** | c'è/ci sono | che/chee **son**o |
| **these** | questi/queste | **kwest**ee/**kwest**ay |
| ***these ones*** | questi(e) qui | **kwest**ee(ay) kwee |
| **thick** | spesso(a) | **spes**-so(a) |
| **thief** | il/la ladro(a) | **lad**ro(a) |
| **thin** (person) | sottile | sot-**teel**ay |
| | magro(a) | **magr**o(a) |
| **thing** | la cosa | **ko**za |
| **to think** | pensare | pen-**sar**ay |

| English | Italian | Pronunciation |
|---|---|---|
| **thirsty**: ***to be thirsty*** | avere sete | a-**vay**ray **say**tay |
| **this** | questo/questa | **kwest**o/ **kwest**a |
| ***this one*** | questo(a) | **kwest**o(a) |
| **those** | quei/quelle/ quegli | kway/**kwel**-lay/ **kwel**yee |
| ***those ones*** | quelli(e) | **kwel**-lee(ay) |
| **throat** | la gola | **gol**a |
| **through** | attraverso | at-tra-**vayr**-so |
| **ticket** (bus, etc), | il biglietto | beel-**yet**-to |
| (entry fee) | il biglietto d'ingresso | beel-**yet**-to deen-**gres**-so |
| ***a single ticket*** | un biglietto di (sola) andata | oon beel-**yet**-to dee (**so**la) an-**dat**a |
| ***a return ticket*** | un biglietto di andata e ritorno | oon beel-**yet**-to dee an-**dat**a ay ree-**tor**no |
| **ticket office** | la biglietteria | beel-yet-tay-**ree**-a |
| **tie** | la cravatta | kra-**vat**-ta |
| **tight** | stretto(a) | **stret**-to(a) |
| **tights** | i collant | ee kol-**lant** |
| **time** | il tempo | **tem**po |
| (of day) | l'ora *f* | **or**a |
| ***what time is it?*** | che ore sono? | kay **or**ay **so**no? |
| ***do you have the time?*** | ha l'ora? | a l**or**a? |
| **timetable** | l'orario *m* | o-**rar**-yo |
| **to tip** (waiter) | dare la mancia | **dar**ay la **man**cha |
| **tired** | stanco(a) | **stan**ko(a) |
| **tissues** | i fazzoletti di carta | fats-so-**let**-tee dee **kar**ta |
| **to** | a | a |
| ***to the airport*** | all'aeroporto | al-la-ayro-**por**to |
| **toast** (to eat) | il pane tostato | **pan**ay tos**ta**to |
| (raising glass) | il brindisi | **breen**-dee-zee |
| **tobacco** | il tabacco | ta-**bak**-ko |
| **tobacconist's** | il tabaccaio | tabak-**ka**-yo |
| **today** | oggi | **od**jee |
| **together** | insieme | een-**syay**may |

# English – Italian

| English | Italian | Pronunciation |
|---|---|---|
| **toilet** | la toilette | twa-**let** |
| **tomato** | il pomodoro | pomo-**dor**o |
| **tomorrow** | domani | do-**ma**nee |
| ***tomorrow morning*** | domani mattina | do-**ma**nee mat-**teen**a |
| ***tomorrow afternoon*** | domani pomeriggio | do-**ma**nee pomay-**reed**-jo |
| ***tomorrow evening*** | domani sera | do-**ma**nee **say**ra |
| **tongue** | la lingua | **leen**-gwa |
| **tonic water** | l'acqua tonica/brillante *f* | **ak**wa **to**neeka/breel-**lan**-tay |
| **tonight** | stasera | sta-**say**ra |
| **too** (also) | anche | **an**kay |
| ***too big*** | troppo grande | **trop**-po **gran**day |
| **toothache** | il mal di denti | mal dee **den**tee |
| **toothbrush** | lo spazzolino da denti | spat-tso-**leen**o da **den**tee |
| **toothpaste** | il dentifricio | dentee-**freech**o |
| **top:** ***the top floor*** | l'ultimo piano *m* | **ool**-teemo **pyan**o |
| **total** | il totale | to-**tal**ay |
| **to touch** | toccare | tok-**kar**ay |
| **tough** (meat) | duro(a) | **door**o(a) |
| **tour** | il giro | **jeer**o |
| **tourist** | il/la turista | too-**reest**a |
| **tourist information** | le informazioni turistiche | eenformats-**yon**ee too-**reest**eekay |
| **tourist office** | l'ufficio turistico *m* | oof-**feech**o too-**reest**eeko |
| **tower** | la torre | **tor**-ray |
| **town** | la città | cheet-**ta** |
| **town centre** | il centro città | **chen**tro cheet-**ta** |
| **toy** | il giocattolo | jo-**kat**-tolo |
| **toy shop** | il negozio di giocattoli | ne-**gots**-yo dee jo-**kat**-tolee |
| **traditional** | tradizionale | tradeets-yo-**nal**ay |
| **traffic** | il traffico | **traf**-feeko |
| **traffic lights** | il semaforo | say-**maf**oro |
| **train** | il treno | **tray**no |
| ***the first train*** | il primo treno | **pree**mo **tray**no |

***the last train*** l'ultimo treno **ool**-teemo **tray**no
***the next train*** il prossimo treno **pros**-seemo **tray**no
**tram** il tram tram
**to transfer** trasferire trasfay-**reer**ay
**to translate** tradurre tra-**door**-ray
**to travel** viaggiare vee-ad-**jar**ay
**travel agent** l'agenzia di viaggi *f* adjen-**tsi**a dee vee-**ad**-jee
**trip** la gita **jee**ta
**trolley** il carrello kar-**rel**-lo
**trousers** i pantaloni panta-**lon**ee
**true** vero(a) **vay**ro(a)
**to try; *to try on*** (clothes, etc) provare pro-**var**ay
**t-shirt** la maglietta mal-**yet**-ta
**to turn** (handle, wheel) girare jee-**rar**ay
**to turn off** (light, etc) spegnere **spen**-yeray
(tap) chiudere **kyoo**-deray
**to turn on** (light, etc) accendere at-**chen**deray
(tap) aprire a-**preer**ay
**twice** due volte; il doppio **doo**ay **vol**tay; **dop**-pyo
**twin-bedded room** una camera a due letti oona **ka**mayra a **doo**ay **le**t-tee
**twin beds** i letti gemelli **let**-tee je-**mel**-lee
**typical** tipico(a) **tee**-peeko(a)

# U

**umbrella** l'ombrello *m* om-**brel**-lo
(sunshade) l'ombrellone *m* om-brayl-**lo**-nay
**uncomfortable** scomodo(a) **sko**-modo(a)
**under** sotto sot-to
**underground** (metro) la metropolitana metro-po-lee-**ta**na
**to understand** capire ka**pee**ray

| | | |
|---|---|---|
| ***I don't understand*** | non capisco | non ka**pee**sko |
| ***do you understand?*** | capisce? | ka**pee**shay? |
| **underwear** | la biancheria intima | byanke**rya** een**teema** |
| **unemployed** | disoccupato(a) | deezok-koo**pa**to(a) |
| **to unfasten** | slacciare | zla-**chya**ray |
| **United Kingdom** | il Regno Unito | **ray**nyo oo**nee**to |
| **United States** | gli Stati Uniti | **sta**tee oo**nee**tee |
| **university** | l'università *f* | oonee-vayr-see**ta** |
| **to unlock** | aprire | a**pree**ray |
| **to unpack** | disfare la valigia | dees-**fa**ray la va-**lee**-ja |
| **unpleasant** | sgradevole | zgra-**day**-volay |
| **until** | fino a | **fee**no a |
| **unusual** | raro(a) | **ra**ro(a) |
| **up:** ***to get up*** | alzarsi | al-**tsar**see |
| **urgent** | urgente | oor**jen**tay |
| **us** | ci; noi | chee; noy |
| **to use** | usare | oo**za**ray |
| **useful** | utile | **oo**teelay |
| **usual** | solito(a) | **so**leeto(a) |
| **usually** | di solito | dee **so**leeto |

## V

| | | |
|---|---|---|
| **vacancy** (in hotel) | la camera libera | **ka**-mayra **lee**bayra |
| **vacant** | libero(a) | **lee**bayro(a) |
| **vacation** | la vacanza | va**kan**tsa |
| **valid** | valido(a) | **va**leedo(a) |
| **valuable** | di valore | dee va**lo**ray |
| **valuables** | gli oggetti di valore | od-**jet**-tee de va**lo**ray |
| **value** | il valore | va**lo**ray |
| **VAT** | l'IVA *f* | **ee**va |
| **vegan** | vegetaliano(a) | vayjayta**lya**no(a) |
| **vegetables** | le verdure | vayr**doo**ray |

| English | Italian | Pronunciation |
|---|---|---|
| **vegetarian** | vegetariano(a) | vayjayta**rya**no(a) |
| **very** | molto | **mol**-to |
| **video camera** | la videocamera | **vee**day-o-**ka**mayra |
| **video cassette/ tape** | la videocassetta | **vee**day-o-kas-**set**-ta |
| **view** | la vista | **vees**-ta |
| **villa** | la villa | **veel**-la |
| **village** | il paese | pa-**ay**zay |
| **vinegar** | l'aceto *m* | a**chay**to |
| **virus** | il virus | **vee**roos |
| **visa** | il visto | **vee**sto |
| **visit** | la visita | **vee**zeeta |
| **to visit** | visitare | veezee**ta**ray |
| **visitor** | il visitatore/ la visitatrice | vee-zee-ta**to**ray/vee-zee-ta**tree**chay |
| **volcano** | il vulcano | vool**ka**no |
| **to vomit** | vomitare | vomee**ta**ray |
| **voucher** | il buono | **bwo**no |

# W

| English | Italian | Pronunciation |
|---|---|---|
| **to wait** (for) | aspettare | as-pet-**ta**ray |
| **waiter/ waitress** | il cameriere/ la cameriera | kamay-**ryay**-ray/ kamay-**ryay**-ra |
| **waiting room** | la sala d'aspetto/ d'attesa | **sa**la das-**pet**-to/ dat-**tay**-sa |
| **to wake up** (someone) | svegliare | zvay-**lya**ray |
| (oneself) | svegliarsi | zvay-**lya**rsee |
| **Wales** | il Galles | **gal**-lays |
| **walk** | la passeggiata | pas-say-**dja**ta |
| **to walk** | andare a piedi | an**da**ray a **pye**dee |
| **wall** | il muro; la parete | **moo**ro; pa**ray**tay |
| **wallet** | il portafoglio | porta**fo**lyo |
| **to want** | volere | vo**lay**ray |
| ***I want...*** | voglio... | **vo**lyo... |
| **warm** | caldo(a) | **kal**-do(a) |
| ***it's warm*** (weather) | fa caldo | fa **kal**-do |

| | | |
|---|---|---|
| **to warm up** (milk, etc) | riscaldare | reeskal**da**ray |
| **to wash** | lavare | la**va**ray |
| (to wash oneself) | lavarsi | la**var**see |
| **wasp sting** | la puntura di vespa | poon**too**ra dee **vays**pa |
| **watch** | l'orologio *m* | oro**lo**jo |
| **to watch** | guardare | gwar**da**ray |
| **water** | l'acqua *f* | **ak**wa |
| ***mineral water*** | l'acqua minerale | **ak**wa meenay**ra**lay |
| ***sparkling/still water*** | l'acqua gassata/ naturale | **ak**wa gas-**sa**ta/ natoo**ra**lay |
| **watermelon** | l'anguria *f* | an**goo**rya |
| **way in** | l'entrata *f*; l'ingresso *m* | ayn**tra**ta; eengrays-so |
| **way out** | l'uscita *f* | oo**shee**ta |
| **we** | noi | noy |
| **weak** (person) | debole | **day**bolay |
| (tea, coffee, etc) | leggero(a) | lay-**djay**ro(a) |
| **to wear** | portare | por**ta**ray |

| | | |
|---|---|---|
| **weather** | il tempo | **tem**po |
| **weather forecast** | le previsioni del tempo | prevee**zyo**nee dayl **tem**po |
| **wedding** | il matrimonio | matree**mo**nyo |
| **week** | la settimana | set-tee**ma**na |
| ***last week*** | la settimana scorsa | la set-tee**ma**na **skor**-sa |
| ***next week*** | la prossima settimana | **pros**-seema set-tee**ma**na |
| ***per week*** | alla settimana | alla set-tee**ma**na |
| ***this week*** | questa settimana | **qways**ta set-tee**ma**na |
| **weekend** | il fine settimana | **fee**nay set-tee**ma**na |
| ***next weekend*** | il prossimo fine settimana | **pros**-seemo **fee**nay set-tee**ma**na |
| ***this weekend*** | questo fine settimana | **qways**to **fee**nay set-tee**ma**na |
| **weekly** | settimanale | set-teema**na**lay |

| English | Italian | Pronunciation |
|---|---|---|
| **to weigh** | pesare | payz**a**ray |
| **weight** | il peso | **pay**zo |
| **welcome** | benvenuto | benvay**noo**to |
| **well** | bene | **be**nay |
| **well-done** (steak) | ben cotto(a) | ben **kot**-to(a) |
| **Welsh** | gallese | gal-**lay**say |
| **west** | ovest | **o**vest |
| **wet** | bagnato(a) | ba**nya**to(a) |
| **what** | cosa | **ko**-za |
| ***what is it?*** | cos'è? | ko-**zay**? |
| **when** | quando | **kwan**do |
| **where** | dove | **do**vay |
| **which** | qual/quale/ quali | kwal/**kwa**lay/ **kwa**lee |
| **while** | mentre | **men**tray |
| ***in a while*** | fra poco | fra **po**ko |
| **whisky** | il whisky *m* | **wee**skee |
| **white** | bianco(a) | **byan**ko(a) |
| **who** | chi | kee |
| **whole** | tutto | **toot**-to |
| **wholemeal bread** | il pane integrale | **pa**nay eentay**gra**lay |
| **whose:** ***whose is it?*** | di chi è? | dee kee ay? |
| **why** | perché | payr**kay** |
| **wife** | la moglie | **mo**lyay |
| **wind** | il vento | **ven**to |
| **window** | la finestra | fee**ne**stra |
| (shop) | la vetrina | ve**tree**na |
| (car) | il finestrino | feenay**stree**no |
| **windy:** ***it's windy*** | c'è vento | chay **ven**to |
| **wine** | il vino | **vee**no |
| ***red wine*** | il vino rosso | **vee**no **ros**-so |
| ***white wine*** | il vino bianco | **vee**no **byan**ko |
| ***dry wine*** | il vino secco | **vee**no **sek**-ko |
| ***sweet wine*** | il vino dolce | **vee**no **dol**chay |
| ***rosé wine*** | il vino rosato | **vee**no ro**za**to |
| ***sparkling wine*** | il vino frizzante | **vee**no free**tsan**tay |
| **winter** | l'inverno *m* | een**ver**no |

**with** con **kon**
*with ice* con ghiaccio kon **gya**chyo
*with milk* con latte kon **lat**-tay
*with sugar* con zucchero kon **tsook**-kayro
**without** senza **sen**tza
*without ice* senza ghiaccio **sen**tza **gya**chyo
*without milk* senza latte **sen**tza **lat**-tay
*without sugar* senza zucchero **sen**tza **tsook**-kayro
**woman** la donna **don**-na
**wonderful** meraviglioso(a) mayravee**lyo**so(a)
**word** la parola pa**ro**la
**work** il lavoro la**vo**ro
**to work** (person) lavorare lavo**ra**ray
(machine, car, etc) funzionare foontsyo**na**ray
**world** il mondo **mon**do
**worried** preoccupato(a) pre-ok-koo**pa**to(a)
**worse** peggio **pe**-djo
**to wrap up** (parcel) incartare eenkar**ta**ray
**to write** scrivere **skree**vayray
*please write it down* lo scriva per favore **skree**va payr fa**vo**ray
**wrong** sbagliato(a) sba**lya**to(a)
*what's wrong?* cosa c'è? **ko**-za chay?

## X

**x-ray** la radiografia radyogra**fee**ya
**to x-ray** radiografare radyogra**fa**ray

## Y

**year** l'anno *m* **an**-no
*last year* l'anno scorso **an**-no **skor**-so
*next year* l'anno prossimo **an**-no **pros**seemo
*this year* quest'anno kwayst-**an**-no
**yearly** (every year) annualmente an-nooal-**meyn**tay
**yellow** giallo(a) **jal**-lo(a)

| | | |
|---|---|---|
| **Yellow Pages** | le pagine gialle® | **pa**jeenay **jal**-lay |
| **yes** | sì | see |
| **yesterday** | ieri | **yay**ree |
| **yet:** ***not yet*** | non ancora | non an-**ko**ra |
| **yoghurt** | lo yogurt | **yo**goort |
| **you** | tu; voi; lei | too; voy; lay |
| **young** | giovane | **jo**vanay |
| **your** | il/la suo(a); il/la tuo(a); il/la vostro(a) | **soo**-o(a); **too**-o(a); **vo**-stro(a) |

## Z

| | | |
|---|---|---|
| **zone** | la zona | **dzo**na |
| **zoo** | lo zoo | dzo-o |

# Italian - English

## A

| Italian | English |
|---|---|
| **a** | at; in |
| **abbiamo...** | we have... |
| ***non abbiamo...*** | we don't have... |
| **abbigliamento** *m* | clothes |
| **abbonamento** *m* | subscription; season ticket |
| **abito** *m* | dress; man's suit |
| **accanto(a)** | beside; next *(to)* |
| **accendere** | to turn on; to light |
| ***accendere i fari*** | switch on your headlights |
| **acceso(a)** | on *(light, engine)* |
| **accettazione** *f* | reception |
| **accomodarsi** | to make oneself comfortable |
| ***si accomodi*** | do take a seat |
| **aceto** *m* | vinegar |
| **ACI** *m* | Automobile Association |
| **acqua** *f* | water |
| ***acqua calda*** | hot water |
| ***acqua gassata*** | sparkling water |
| ***acqua minerale*** | mineral water |
| ***acqua naturale*** | still water |
| ***acqua potabile*** | drinking water |
| **adesso** | now |
| **aereo** *m* | plane; aircraft |
| **aeroporto** *m* | airport |
| **affari** *mpl* | business |
| **affittare** | to rent; to let |
| **agenzia di viaggi** *f* | travel agent |
| **aggredire** | to attack |
| **aiutare** | to help |
| **aiuto!** | help! |
| **albergo** *m* | hotel |
| **alcuni(e)** | some; a few |
| **alcuno(a)** | any; some |
| **alimentari** *mpl* | groceries |
| **allarme antincendio** *m* | fire alarm |
| **allergia** *f* | allergy |
| **allergico(a)** | allergic to |
| **alloggio** *m* | accommodation |
| **alt** | stop |
| **alto(a)** | high; tall |
| ***alta stagione*** | high season |
| **altro(a)** | other |
| ***altri passaporti*** | other passports |
| **alzarsi** | to get up |
| **amare** | to love *(person)* |
| **amaro(a)** | bitter *(taste)* |
| **ambasciata** *f* | embassy |
| **ambulatorio** *m* | surgery; out-patients |
| **amico(a)** *m/f* | friend |
| **ammalato(a)** | ill |
| **ammontare** *m* | total amount |

| | |
|---|---|
| **analisi del sangue** *f* | blood test |
| **analgesico** *m* | painkiller |
| **anche** | too; also; even |
| **ancora** | still; yet; again |
| ***ancora un po'?*** | a little more? |
| **andare** | to go |
| ***andare a piedi*** | to go on foot |
| ***andare bene*** | to fit *(clothes)* |
| **andata:** ***andata e ritorno*** | return *(ticket)* |
| ***di (sola) andata*** | single *(ticket)* |
| **andiamo!** | let's go! |
| ***andiamo a...*** | we're going to... |
| **anno** *m* | year |
| ***buon anno!*** | happy New Year! |
| **annullare** | to cancel |
| **annuncio** *m* | announcement; advert |
| **anticipo** *m* | advance *(loan)* |
| ***in anticipo*** | in advance; early |
| **anticoncezionale** *m* | contraceptive |
| **antifurto** *m* | burglar alarm |
| **anziano(a)** *m/f* | senior citizen |
| **aperto(a)** | open |
| ***all'aperto*** | open-air |
| **appartamento** *m* | flat; apartment |
| **appuntamento** *m* | appointment; date |
| **apribottiglie** *m* | bottle opener |
| **aprire** | to open; to turn on *(tap)* |
| **apriscatole** *m* | tin-opener |
| **aranciata** *f* | orangeade |
| **area di servizio** *f* | service area |
| **aria condizionata** *f* | air-conditioning |
| **arredato(a)** | furnished |
| **arrivare** | to arrive |
| **arrivederci** | goodbye |
| **arrivo** *m* | arrival |
| **articoli da dichiarare** *mpl* | goods to declare |
| **articoli da regalo** *mpl* | gifts |
| **asciugamano** *m* | towel |
| **asciugare** | to dry |
| **ASL** | local health centre |
| **ascoltare** | to listen *(to)* |
| **asma** *f* | asthma |
| **aspettare** | to wait *(for)*; to expect |
| **assaggiare** | to taste |
| **assegno** *m* | cheque |
| **assicurato(a)** | insured |
| **assicurazione** *f* | insurance |
| **assistenza** *f* | assistance; aid |
| **assorbenti** *mpl* | sanitary towels |

# Italian – English

***assorbenti interni*** tampons
**attaccare** to attach; to attack; to fasten
**attendere** to wait for
**attento(a)** careful
**attenzione** *f* caution
***fare attenzione*** to be careful
**atterrare** to land *(plane)*
**attraversare** to cross
**attraverso** through
**attrezzatura** *f* equipment
**auguri!** best wishes!
**aumentare** to increase
**auto** *f* car
**autobus** *m* bus
**autofficina** *f* garage *(for repairs)*
**autonoleggio** *m* car hire
**autorimessa** *f* garage

**autostop** *m* hitchhiking
**autostrada** *f* motorway
**avanti!** come in!
**avere** to have
***avere bisogno di*** to need
***avere fame*** to be hungry
***avere sete*** to be thirsty
**avvisare** to inform; to warn
**avviso** *m* notice
**azienda di soggiorno** *f* local tourist board
**Azienda Sanitaria Locale** local health centre
**azzurro(a)** light blue

## B

**bagagliaio** *m* boot (of car)
**bagaglio a mano** *m* hand luggage

**bagno** *m* bath; bathroom
**ballare** to dance
**balsamo** *m* hair conditioner
**bambino(a)** *m/f* child; baby
**bambini** *mpl* children
**banca** *f* bank
**bancarella** *f* stall; stand
**banco** *m* counter; desk
**banco informazioni** enquiry desk
**Bancomat®** *m* cash dispenser
**basso(a)** low; short
**basta** that's enough
**battello** *m* boat
**batteria** *f* battery *(car)*
***batteria scarica*** flat battery
**bello(a)** beautiful; fine; lovely
**bene** well; all right; OK
**benvenuto** welcome
**benzina** *f* petrol

**bere** to drink
**bianco(a)** white; blank
***lasciate in bianco*** leave blank
**bibita** *f* soft drink
**bicchiere** *m* glass (*drinking*)
**bicicletta** *f* bicycle
**biglietteria** *f* ticket office
**biglietto** *m* ticket; note; card
**binario** *m* platform
**biologico(a)** organic
**biondo(a)** blond (*person*)
**birra** *f* beer
***birra alla spina*** draught beer
***birra bionda*** lager
**birreria** *f* bar; pub
**bisogno** *m* need
***avere bisogno di*** to need
**blocchetto di biglietti** *m* book of tickets
**blu** blue

**bocca** *f* mouth
**bollire** to boil
**bollitore** *m* kettle
**bombola del gas** *f* gas cylinder
**borsa** *f* bag; handbag; briefcase
**borsellino** *m* purse; wallet
**botteghino** *m* box office
**bottiglia** *f* bottle
**braccio** *m* arm
**britannico(a)** British
**bruciare** to burn
**brutto(a)** bad (*weather, news*); ugly
**buca delle lettere** *f* postbox
**buono(a)** good
***buon appetito!*** enjoy your meal!
***buon compleanno!*** happy birthday!

***buon giorno*** good morning/afternoon
***buona notte*** good night
***buona sera*** good afternoon/evening
***a buon mercato*** cheap
**buono** *m* voucher; coupon; token
**burro di cacao** *m* lip salve
**bustina di tè** *f* tea bag
**buttare via** to throw away

## C

**cabina telefonica** *f* phonebox
**cadere** to fall
**caffè** *m* coffee (*espresso*)
***caffè solubile*** instant coffee
***caffellatte*** milky coffee
**calcolatrice** *f* calculator

# Italian – English

**caldo(a)** hot
**calmante** *m* sedative
**calmo(a)** calm
**calzature** *fpl* shoeshop
**calze** *fpl* stockings
**calzini** *mpl* socks
**calzolaio** *m* shoe mender
**cambiare** to change
***cambiare autobus/soldi*** to change bus/money
**cambiarsi** to change one's clothes
**cambio** *m* exchange; gear
**camera** *f* room *(in house, hotel)*
***camera da letto*** bedroom
***camera libera*** vacancy *(in hotel)*
***camera per famiglia*** family room
***camera singola/doppia*** single/double room
**cameriera** *f* chambermaid
**cameriere** *m* waiter
**camion** *m* lorry
**camminare** to walk
**campanello** *m* bell
**campeggio** *m* camping; campsite
**campo da tennis** *m* tennis court
**campo di calcio** *m* football pitch
**cancellare** to erase; to cancel
**cancellazione** *f* cancellation
**cane** *m* dog
**cannuccia** *f* straw *(for drinking)*
**canotto** *m* dinghy *(rubber)*
**cantare** to sing
**capelli** *mpl* hair
**capire** to understand
***capisce?*** do you understand?
***non capisco*** I don't understand
**capitale** *f* capital *(city)*
**Capodanno** *m* New Year's day
**capolinea** *m* terminus
**carabiniere** *m* policeman
**carburante** *m* fuel
**carburatore** *m* carburettor
**caricare** to charge *(battery)*
**carico** *m* load; shipment
**carino(a)** pretty; lovely; nice
**carne** *f* meat
**caro(a)** dear; expensive
**carrello** *m* trolley
**carro attrezzi** *m* breakdown van

**carrozza letto** *f* sleeper
**carrozzeria** *f* bodywork
**carta assegni** *f* cheque card
***carta di credito*** *f* credit card
***carta d'identità*** *f* identity card
***carta igienica*** *f* toilet paper
***carta stradale*** *f* road map
***carta verde*** *f* green card
**cartello** *m* sign; signpost
**cartolina** *f* postcard
**casa** *f* house; home
**casalinghi** *mpl* household articles
**casco** *m* helmet
**casella postale** *f* post-office box
**caso:** ***in caso di*** in case of
**cassa** *f* till; cash desk
**cassaforte** *f* safe *(for valuables)*
**cassetta delle lettere** *f* letterbox
**cassiere(a)** *m/f* cashier; teller
**catene (da neve)** *fpl* (snow) chains
**cattivo(a)** bad; nasty; naughty
**causa** *f* cause; case *(lawsuit)*
**a causa di** because of
**cavalcare** to ride *(horse)*
**cavallo** *m* horse
**cavo da rimorchio** *m* tow rope
**c'è** there is
**cellulare** *m* mobile phone
**cena** *f* dinner *(evening)*
**cenare** to have dinner
**centesimo** *m* cent *(euro)*
**cento** hundred
**centro città** *m* city centre
**centro commerciale** *m* shopping centre
**centro storico** *m* old town
**ceppo bloccaruote** *m* wheel clamp
**cercare** to look for
**che** what; who; which
***che gusto?*** what flavour?
***che ore sono?*** what time is it?
**chi?** who?
***di chi è?*** whose is it?
**chiamare** to call
**chiamarsi** to be called *(name)*
***come si chiama?*** what's your name?
**chiamata** *f* call *(telephone)*
**chiave** *f* key
**chiedere** to ask; to ask for
**chiesa** *f* church

# Italian – English

| Italian | English |
|---|---|
| **chilo** *m* | kilo |
| **chiudere** | to close; to turn off *(tap)* |
| ***chiudere a chiave*** | to lock |
| **chiuso(a)** | closed |
| ***chiuso per turno*** | closed for weekly day off |
| ***chiuso per ferie*** | closed for holidays |
| **ciao!** | hi!; bye! |
| **cintura di sicurezza** *f* | seatbelt |
| **cioccolato** *m* | chocolate |
| **circolazione** *f* | traffic |
| **circonvallazione** | ring road |
| **citofono** *m* | intercom |
| **città** *f* | city; town |
| **cittadino(a)** | citizen |
| **climatizzato(a)** | air-conditioned |
| **codice** *m* | code |
| ***codice a barre*** | barcode |
| ***codice postale*** | postcode |
| **cognome** *m* | surname |
| ***di cognome mi chiamo...*** | my surname is... |
| **coincidenza** *f* | connection *(train, etc)*; coincidence |
| **colazione** *f* | breakfast; lunch |
| **colore** *m* | colour |
| **colpa** *f* | fault |
| ***non è colpa mia*** | it's not my fault |
| **come** | like; as; how |
| ***come?*** | how? |
| ***come si chiama?*** | what's your name? |
| ***come si pronuncia?*** | how is it pronounced? |
| ***come si scrive?*** | how is it spelt? |
| ***come sta?*** | how are you? |
| ***come va?*** | how's it going? |
| **cominciare** | to begin |
| **commissariato** *m* | police station |
| **compagnia aerea** *f* | airline |
| **compilare** | to fill in *(form)* |
| **compleanno** *m* | birthday |
| **completo(a)** | no vacancies; full |
| **comprare** | to buy |
| **compreso(a)** | included |
| **con** | with |
| ***con bagno*** | with bathroom |
| **confermare** | to confirm |
| **congelatore** *m* | freezer |
| **cono gelato** *m* | ice-cream cone |
| **conoscere** | to know *(to be acquainted with)* |
| **conservante** *m* | preservative |
| **consigliare** | to advise |
| **consiglio** *m* | advice |
| **consumare** | to use up |

| Italian | English |
|---|---|
| ***da consumarsi entro*** | best before |
| **contanti** *mpl* | cash |
| ***pagare in contanti*** | to pay cash |
| **continuare** | to continue |
| **conto** *m* | account; bill |
| ***conto corrente*** | current account |
| **contorno** *m* | vegetable side dish |
| **contravvenzione** *f* | fine |
| **contro** | against; versus |
| **controllare** | to check |
| **convalidare** | to validate *(ticket)* |
| **coppia** *f* | couple *(two people)* |
| **corrente** *f* | current *(electric, water)* |
| **correre** | to run |
| **corsa** *f* | race; journey |
| ***corsa semplice*** | single fare |
| **corsia** *f* | lane; hospital ward; route |
| ***corsia di emergenza*** | hard shoulder |
| ***corsia di sorpasso*** | outside lane |
| **corto(a)** | short |
| **cos'è?** | what is it? |
| ***cos'è successo?*** | what happened? |
| **cosa** *f* | thing |
| ***cosa?*** | what? |
| **così** | so, thus |
| **costare** | to cost |
| **costoso(a)** | expensive |
| **costruire** | to build |
| **cotto(a)** | cooked |
| ***poco cotto(a)*** | medium rare *(steak)* |
| **credere** | to believe |
| **credito** *m* | credit |
| ***non si fa credito*** | no credit given |
| **crema da barba** *f* | shaving cream |
| **crescere** | to grow |
| **cric** *m* | jack *(for car)* |
| **crisi epilettica** *f* | epileptic fit |
| **crocevia** *m* | crossroads |
| **crudo(a)** | raw |
| **cucchiaio** *m* | spoon; tablespoon |
| **cucina** *f* | cooker; kitchen; cooking |
| **cucinare** | to cook |
| **cuffie** *fpl* | earphones |
| **cuocere** | to cook |
| **cuoio** *m* | leather |
| **curva** *f* | bend; corner |
| **custodia** *f* | case; holder |

# Italian - English

## D

| | |
|---|---|
| **da** | from; by; worth |
| ***da asporto*** | take-away |
| ***da vedere*** | worth seeing |
| **danneggiare** | to spoil; to damage |
| **danno** *m* | damage |
| **dare** | to give |
| ***dare la precedenza*** | give way |
| ***dare la mancia*** | to tip (*waiter, etc*) |
| **data** *f* | date |
| ***data di nascita*** | date of birth |
| ***data di scadenza*** | sell-by date |
| **davanti a** | in front of; opposite |
| **debito** *m* | debt |
| **decollare** | to take off (*plane*) |
| **delizioso(a)** | delicious |
| **dentifricio** *m* | toothpaste |
| **dentro** | in; indoors; inside |
| **descrivere** | to describe |
| **desiderare** | to want; to desire |
| **destra** *f* | right |
| **detersivo** *m* | detergent |
| **detrazione** *f* | deduction |
| **deviazione** *f* | detour; diversion |
| **di** | of; some |
| ***di cristallo/plastica*** | made of crystal/plastic |
| ***di lusso*** | luxury (*hotel, etc*) |
| ***di mattina*** | in the morning |
| ***di pomeriggio*** | in the afternoon |
| ***di notte*** | at night |
| ***di stagione*** | in season |
| **dichiarare** | to declare |
| **dieta** *f* | diet |
| ***essere a dieta*** | to be on a diet |
| **dietro** | behind; after |
| **difficile** | difficult |
| **dimenticare** | to forget |
| **dire** | to say; to tell |
| **diretto(a)** | direct |
| ***treno diretto*** | through train |
| **direttore** *m* | manager; director |
| **direzione** *f* | management; direction |
| **disco orario** *m* | parking disk |
| **disdire** | to cancel |
| **dispiacere:** | |
| ***mi dispiace*** | I'm sorry |
| **disponibile** | available |
| **distanza** *f* | distance |
| **distributore di benzina** *m* | petrol station |

| | |
|---|---|
| **disturbare** | to disturb |
| **ditta** *f* | firm; company |
| **divano letto** *m* | sofa bed |
| **diversi(e)** | several; various |
| **diverso(a)** | different |
| **divertente** | funny (*amusing*) |
| **divertirsi** | to enjoy oneself |
| **dividere** | to share |
| **divieto** | forbidden |
| ***divieto di sorpasso*** | no overtaking |
| ***divieto di sosta*** | no parking |
| **doccia** *f* | shower |
| **documenti** *mpl* | papers (*passport*) |
| **dogana** *f* | customs |
| **dolce** | sweet (*not savoury*); mild |
| **doloroso(a)** | painful |
| **domanda** *f* | question |
| **domandare** | to ask (*question*) |
| **domani** | tomorrow |
| ***domani mattina*** | tomorrow morning |
| ***domani pomeriggio*** | tomorrow afternoon |
| ***domani sera*** | tomorrow evening/night |
| **donna** *f* | woman |
| **dopo** | after; afterward(s) |
| **dopodomani** | the day after tomorrow |
| **doppio(a)** | double |
| **dormire** | to sleep |
| **dove?** | where? |
| **dovere** | to have to |
| **dritto(a)** | straight |
| ***sempre dritto*** | straight on |
| **durante** | during |
| **durare** | to last |
| **duro(a)** | hard; tough; harsh |

## E

| | |
|---|---|
| **e** | and |
| **è** | is (*to be*) |
| **eccesso** *m* | excess |
| **eccezionale** | exceptional |
| **eccezione** *f* | exception |
| **ecco** | here is/are |
| **economico(a)** | cheap |
| **effetti personali** *mpl* | belongings |
| **elenco** *m* | list |
| ***elenco telefonico*** | phone directory |
| **elettricità** *f* | electricity |
| **elettrico(a)** | electric(al) |
| **emergenza** *f* | emergency |
| **entrambi(e)** | both |
| **entrare** | to come/go in; to enter |
| **entrata** *f* | entrance |
| ***entrata libera*** | free admission |

# Italian – English

| | |
|---|---|
| **errore** *m* | mistake |
| **esaurito(a)** | exhausted; out of print |
| ***tutto esaurito*** | sold out |
| **escluso(a)** | excluding |
| **esente** | exempt |
| **esempio** *m* | example |
| **esperto(a)** | expert; experienced |
| **esportare** | to export |
| **essere** | to be |
| ***essere capace (di)*** | to be able *(to)* |
| ***essere d'accordo*** | to agree |
| **est** *m* | east |
| **esterno(a)** | outside; external |
| **estero(a)** | foreign |
| ***all'estero*** | abroad |
| **età** *f* | age |
| **eventuale** | possible |
| **evitare** | to avoid |

## F

| | |
|---|---|
| **fa** | ago |
| **fabbricare** | to manufacture |
| **faccia** *f* | face |
| **facile** | easy |
| **fallire** | to fail |
| **falso(a)** | fake |
| **fame** *f* | hunger |
| ***avere fame*** | to be hungry |
| **famiglia** *f* | family |
| **familiare** | family; familiar |
| **fare** | to do; to make |
| ***fare attenzione*** | to be careful |
| ***fare la spesa*** | to go shopping |
| **farmacia** *f* | chemist's; pharmacy |
| ***farmacie di turno*** | duty chemists |
| **fastidio: *non mi dà fastidio*** | I don't mind |
| **fatto(a) a mano** | hand-made |
| **fatto di...** | made of... |
| **fattura** *f* | invoice |
| **favore** *m* | favour |
| ***per favore*** | please |
| **fazzoletto** *m* | handkerchief |
| ***fazzoletto di carta*** | tissue |
| **febbre** *f* | |
| ***avere la febbre*** | to have a temperature |
| **felice** | happy |
| **feriale** | workday (Mon.-Sat.) |
| **ferie** *fpl* | holiday(s) |
| ***essere in ferie*** | to be on holiday |
| **ferire** | to injure |
| **ferita** *f* | wound; injury; cut |
| **fermare** | to stop |
| **fermata** *f* | stop |

**fermo(a)** still; off *(machine)*
***stare fermo*** to stay still
**ferrovia** *f* railway
**festa nazionale** *f* public holiday
**festivo(a)** Sunday/public holiday
**figlia** *f* daughter
**figlio** *m* son
**fila** *f* line *(row, queue)*
***fare la fila*** to queue
**fine** *f* end
***fine settimana*** *m* weekend
**finestra** *f* window
**finestrino** *m* window *(car, train)*
**finire** to finish
**finito(a)** finished
**fino a** until; as far as
***fino alle due*** till 2 o'clock
**fiori** *mpl* flowers
**firma** *f* signature
***firmare*** to sign
**fon** *m* hairdryer
**fondo** *m* back *(of room)*; bottom
**forbici** *fpl* scissors
**forchetta** *f* fork *(for eating)*
**formaggio** *m* cheese
**forno** *m* oven
***forno a microonde*** microwave
**forse** perhaps
**forte** strong; loud; high *(speed)*
**fortunato(a)** lucky
**forza** *f* strength; force
**fotocopia** *f* photocopy
**fotocopiare** to photocopy
**fototessera** *f* passport-type photo
**fra** between; among(st)
***fra due giorni*** in 2 days
***fra poco*** in a while
**francobollo** *m* stamp
**fratello** *m* brother
**freddo(a)** cold
**frenare** to brake
**freno** *m* brake
**fretta** *f* hurry
***avere fretta*** to be in a hurry
**friggere** to fry
**frigorifero** *m* refrigerator
**frizzante** fizzy; sparkling
**fronte** *f* forehead; front
***di fronte a*** facing; opposite
**frutta** *f* fruit
**fuggire** to escape
**fumare** to smoke

***non fumo*** I don't smoke
**fumo** *m* smoke
**funzionare** to work *(mechanism)*
***non funziona*** it doesn't work
**fuori** outside; out
**fuori servizio** out of order
**furto** *m* theft

## G

**gabinetto** *m* lavatory
**galleria** *f* tunnel; gallery; arcade; circle *(theatre)*
**gamba** *f* leg
**garanzia** *f* guarantee
**gasolio** *m* diesel
**gassato(a)** fizzy
**gassosa** *f* lemonade
**gatto** *m* cat
**gelateria** *f* ice-cream shop
**geloso(a)** jealous
**genere** *m* kind *(type)*; gender
**genitori** *mpl* parents
**gentile** kind *(person)*
**gettare** to throw
**ghiaccio** *m* ice
**ghiacciolo** *m* ice lolly
**giacca** *f* jacket
**giallo** *m* thriller
**giallo(a)** yellow; amber *(light)*
**giardino** *m* garden
**giocare** to play; to gamble
**gioco** *m* game
**gioielleria** *f* jeweller's
**gioielli** *mpl* jewellery
**giornalaio** *m* newsagent
**giornale** *m* newspaper
**giorno** *m* day
***giorni feriali*** Monday-Saturday
***giorni festivi*** Sundays/holidays
**giovane** young
**girare** to turn; to spin
**giro turistico** *m* sightseeing tour
**gita** *f* trip; excursion
**giù** down; downstairs
**giusto(a)** fair; right *(correct)*
**gli** the; to him/it
**gomma** *f* rubber; tyre
***gomma a terra*** flat tyre
**gonfio(a)** swollen
**gonna** *f* skirt
**gradevole** pleasant
**grana** *f* parmesan cheese
**grande** large; great; big

**grande magazzino** *m* department store
**grasso(a)** fat; greasy
**gratis, gratuito(a)** free of charge
***il servizio è gratuito*** service included
**grave** serious
**grazie** thank you
**gridare** to shout
**grigio(a)** grey
**griglia** *f* grill
**grosso(a)** big; thick
**gruppo** *m* group
**guadagnare** to earn
**guardare** to look *(at)*; to watch
**guardia** *f* guard
**guasto** out of order
**guida** *f* guide *(person or book)*; directory
***guida telefonica*** telephone directory
***guida turistica*** tour guide
**guidare** to drive; to steer
**guidatore** *m* driver
**gusto** *m* flavour

## H

**ha...?** do you have...?
***ha l'ora?*** do you have the time?
**ho...** I have...
***ho ... anni*** I'm ... years old
***ho bisogno di...*** I need...
***ho fame*** I'm hungry
***ho fretta*** I'm in a hurry
***ho sete*** I'm thirsty

## I

**i** the *(plural)*
**identificare** to identify
**ieri** yesterday
**il** the *(singular)*
**imbarco** *m* boarding
***carta d'imbarco*** *f* boarding card
**immediatamente** at once
**immondizie** *fpl* rubbish
**imparare** to learn
**importare** to import; to matter
***non importa*** it doesn't matter
**imposta** *f* tax *(on income)*; shutter
**improbabile** unlikely
**in** in; to
***in vacanza*** on holiday
**incantevole** charming
**incartare** to wrap up *(parcel)*

# Italian - English

**incassare** to cash *(a cheque)*
**incidente** *m* accident
**incluso(a)** included; enclosed
**incontrare** to meet
**incrocio** *m* crossroads; junction
**indicazioni** *fpl* directions
**indietro** backwards; behind
**indirizzo** *m* address
**infatti** in fact; actually
**infiammabile** inflammable
**informare** to inform
***informarsi (di)*** to enquire *(about)*
**informazioni** *fpl* information
**Inghilterra** *f* England
**inglese** English
**ingorgo stradale** *m* traffic jam
**ingresso** *m* entry/entrance
***ingresso gratuito*** free entry
**inizio** *m* start
**inoltre** besides
**insegnante** *m/f* teacher
**insegnare** to teach
**inserire** to insert
**insieme** together
**interessante** interesting
**interno** *m* inside; extension *(phone)*
**intero(a)** whole
**intorno** around
**introdurre** to introduce
**inutile** unnecessary; useless
**invalido(a)** disabled; invalid
**invece di** instead of
**inverno** *m* winter
**inviare** to send
**invitare** to invite
**invito** *m* invitation
**io** I
**Irlanda** *f* Ireland
**irlandese** Irish
**iscriversi a** to join *(club)*
**iscrizione** *f* inscription; enrolment
**istruzioni** *fpl* instructions
**Italia** *f* Italy
**italiano(a)** Italian
**IVA** *f* VAT

## L

**la** the; her; it; you
**là** there
***per di là*** that way
**labbra** *fpl* lips
**ladro** *m* thief
**lampada** *f* lamp

**lana** *f* wool
**largo(a)** wide; broad
**lasciare** to leave; to let *(allow)*
**lassù** up there
**latte** *m* milk
***latte intero*** whole milk
***latte scremato*** skimmed milk
**lavabile** washable
**lavanderia** *f* laundry *(place)*
**lavare** to wash
**lavarsi** to wash *(oneself)*
**lavasecco** *m* dry-cleaner's
**lavatrice** *f* washing machine
**lavorare** to work *(person)*
**lavoro** *m* job; occupation; work
**le** the; them; to her; to you
**leggere** to read
**leggero(a)** light *(not heavy)*; weak
**lei** she; her; you
**lentamente** slowly
**lente** *f* lens *(of glasses)*
***lenti a contatto*** *fpl* contact lenses
**lento** slow
**letto** *m* bed
**lettore CD** *m* CD player
**lì** there *(over there)*
**libero(a)** free/vacant
**libretto degli assegni** *m* cheque book
**libro** *m* book
**linea** *f* line; route
**liquido** *m* liquid
**liscio(a)** smooth; straight; plain
**listino prezzi** *m* price list
**litro** *m* litre
**lo** him; it
**locale** *m* room; place; local train
**località di vacanza** *f* resort
**Londra** *f* London
**lontano(a)** far
**lozione** *f* lotion
**luce** *f* light
**luglio** *m* July
**lui** he/him
**lunedì** *m* Monday
**lunghezza** *f* length
**lungo(a)** long
***lungo la strada*** along the street
***a lungo*** for a long time
**luogo** *m* place
**lusso** *m* luxury

## M

**ma** but
**macchina** *f* car; machine
***macchina fotografica*** *f* camera
**madre** *f* mother
**magazzino** *m* warehouse
**maggio** *m* May
**maggiore** larger; greater; older; largest; greatest; oldest
**magro(a)** thin *(person)*; low-fat; lean *(meat)*
**mai** never; ever
**mal** *see* **male**
**malato(a)** ill; sick
**malattia** *f* disease
**male** badly *(not well)*
**male** *m* pain; ache
***mal di testa*** headache
**maltempo** *m* bad weather
**mamma** *f* mum(my)
**mancia** *f* tip *(to waiter, etc)*
**mandare** to send
**mangiare** to eat
**mano** *f* hand
**marca** *f* brand *(make)*
**mare** *m* sea; seaside
**marito** *m* husband
**marrone** *m* brown; chestnut
**martedì** *m* Tuesday
**marzo** *m* March
**maschile** masculine; male
**massimo(a)** maximum
**masticare** to chew
**materiale** *m* material
**matrimonio** *m* wedding
**mattina** *f* morning
**matto(a)** mad
**meccanico** *m* mechanic; repair shop
**medicina** *f* medicine
**medico** *m* doctor
**meglio** better; best
**meno** less; minus
**mensile, mensilmente** monthly
**mento** *m* chin
**mentre** while; whereas
**meraviglioso(a)** wonderful
**mercato** *m* market
**merce** *f* goods
**mercoledì** *m* Wednesday
**mese** *m* month
**messaggio** *m* message
**metà** *f* half
**metro** *m* metre
**metropolitana** *f* underground; metro

**mettere** to put; to put on *(clothes)*
**mezzi** *mpl* means; transport
**mezzo** *m* middle
**mezzo(a)** half
**mezz'ora** *f* half an hour
**mi** me; to me; myself
**mia** my (*f*)
**migliorare** to improve
**migliore** better; best
**miliardo** *m* billion
**mille** thousand
**minimo** *m* minimum
**minorenne** underage
**minori** *mpl* minors
**mio** my (*m*)
**modo** *m* way; manner
**modulo** *m* form *(document)*
**moglie** *f* wife
**molti(e)** many
***molte grazie*** thanks very much
**molto** much; a lot; very
**moneta** *f* coin; currency
**montagna** *f* mountain
**morire** to die
**morto(a)** dead
**mosca** *f* fly
**mostra** *f* exhibition
**mostrare** to show
**motore** *m* engine; motor
**multa** *f* fine *(to be paid)*
**municipio** *m* town hall
**museo** *m* museum
**musica** *f* music

## N

**N** north *(abbreviation)*
**nascita** *f* birth
**nato(a)** born
**nave** *f* ship
**nazionale** national; domestic *(flight)*
**nazione** *f* nation
**né ... né** neither ... nor
**necessario(a)** necessary
**negozio** *m* shop
**nero(a)** black
**nessuno(a)** no; nobody; none
**nevicare** to snow
**niente** nothing
**nipotina** *f* granddaughter
**nipotino** *m* grandson
**nocivo(a)** harmful
**noi** we
**noleggiare** to hire
**nome** *m* name; first name
**non** not

# Italian – English

***non c'è*** there isn't
***non funziona*** it doesn't work
***non capisco*** I don't understand
**nonna** *f* grandmother
**nonno** *m* grandfather
**nord** *m* north
**nostro(a)** our
**notizie** *fpl* news
**notte** *f* night
**novembre** *m* November
**nulla** nothing
**numero** *m* number; size (*of shoe*)
**nuotare** to swim
**nuovo(a)** new
**nuvoloso(a)** cloudy

## O

**o** or
**O** west (*abbr. for Ovest*)
**obbligatorio(a)** compulsory
**occasione** *f* opportunity; bargain
**occhiali** *mpl* glasses
**occhio** *m* eye
**occupato(a)** busy/engaged
**oggetto** *m* object
**oggi** today
**ogni** each; every
***ogni quanto?*** how often?
**oltre** beyond; besides
**ombra** *f* shade
**ombrello** *m* umbrella
**onestà** *f* honesty
**onesto(a)** honest
**operatore turistico** *m* tour operator
**opuscolo** *m* brochure
**ora** *f* now; hour
***che ore sono?*** what's the time?
**orario** *m* timetable
***in orario*** on time
**ordinare** to order; to prescribe
**ordine** *f* order (*in restaurant*)
**ordinato(a)** tidy
**orecchio** *m* ear
**oreficeria** *f* jeweller's
**oro** *m* gold
**orologeria** *m* watchmaker's
**orologio** *m* clock; watch
**ospedale** *m* hospital
**ospite** *m/f* guest; host/hostess
**ottenere** to get; obtain
**ottimo(a)** excellent
**ottobre** *m* October
**ovest** *m* west

## P

**pacchetto** *m* packet
**padre** *m* father
**paese** *m* country *(nation)*; village
**pagare** to pay; to pay for
**pagato(a)** paid
**pagina** *f* page
**paio** *m* pair
**palazzo** *m* building; block of flats; palace
**palla** *f* ball
**pane** *m* bread; loaf
***pane integrale*** wholemeal bread
**panetteria** *f* baker's
**panino** *m* bread roll
**papa** *m* pope
**papà** *m* daddy
**parcheggiare** to park
**parcheggio** *m* car park
**parco** *m* park
**parente** *m/f* relation; relative
**parlare** to speak; to talk
**parola** *f* word
**parrucchiere(a)** *m/f* hairdresser
**parte** *f* share; part; side
**partenza** *f* departures
**partire** to depart; to leave
**partita** *f* match; game
**passaporto** *m* passport
**passeggiata** *f* walk; stroll
**pasticcino** *m* cake *(small, fancy)*
**pastiglia** *f* tablet *(pill)*
**pasto** *m* meal
**pastorizzato** pasteurised
**patente** *f* permit; driving licence
**paziente** *m/f* patient
**pedaggio** *m* toll *(motorway)*
**pedoni** *mpl* pedestrians
**peggio** worse
**pelle** *f* skin; hide; leather
**pelletterie** *fpl* leather goods
**penna** *f* pen
**pensare** to think
**pensione** *f* guesthouse
**per** for; per; in order to
***per esempio*** for example
***per favore*** please
**perché** why; because; so that
**perdere** to lose; to miss *(train, etc)*
**perdita** *f* leak *(of gas, liquid)*

# Italian - English

**pericolo** *m* danger
**pericoloso(a)** dangerous
**permesso** *m* licence; permit
***permesso!*** excuse me! *(to get by)*
**permettere** to allow
**perso(a)** lost *(object)*; missed *(train)*
**persona** *f* person
**pesante** heavy
**pesare** to weigh
**peso** *m* weight
**petto** *m* chest; breast
**pezzo** *m* piece; bit; cut *(of meat)*
**piacere** to please
***le piace?*** do you like it?
***piacere!*** pleased to meet you!
**piangere** to cry *(weep)*
**piano** slowly; quietly
**pianta** *f* map; plan; plant
**piatto** *m* dish; course; plate
**piazza** *f* square *(in town)*
**piccante** spicy; hot
**piccolo(a)** little; small
**piede** *m* foot
***a piedi*** on foot
**pieno(a)** full
**pigiama** *m* pyjamas
**pigro(a)** lazy
**pioggia** *f* rain
**piovere** to rain
**piscina** *f* swimming pool
**più** more; most; plus
***più di*** more than
**plastica** *f* plastic
**po'**: ***un po'*** a little
**pochi(e)** few
**poco(a)** little; not much
**poi** then
**polizia** *f* police
**poliziotto** *m* policeman
**poltrona** *f* armchair; seat in stalls
**pomeriggio** *m* afternoon
**ponte** *m* bridge; deck
**porta** *f* door; gate; goal
**portafoglio** *m* wallet
**portare** to carry/bring; to wear
**porto** *m* port; harbour
**porzione** *f* portion; helping
**possiamo** we can
***non possiamo*** we cannot
**posso** I can
***non posso*** I cannot
**posta** *f* post office; mail
**posteggio** *m* car park
**posto** *m* place; job; seat
**potabile** safe to drink

**potere** to be able
**pranzo** *m* lunch
**predeterminare l'importo desiderato** select required amount
**preferire** to prefer
**preferito(a)** favourite
**prefisso** *m* prefix; area code
**pregare** to pray
***si prega...*** please...
**prego** don't mention it!
**premere** to push; to press
**premio** *m* prize
**prendere** to take; to catch (*bus, etc*)
**prenotare** to reserve
**prenotazione** *f* reservation
**preoccupato(a)** worried
**preparare** to prepare; to get ready
**prestare** to lend
**presto** early; soon
**prezzo** *m* price
**prima di** before
**primavera** *f* spring (*season*)
**primo(a)** first; top; early
**principale** main
**privato(a)** private
**professione** *f* profession
**profondità** *f* depth
**profondo(a)** deep
**proibire** to ban; to prohibit
**proibito(a)** forbidden; prohibited
**promettere** to promise
**pronto(a)** ready
***pronto!*** hello! (*on telephone*)
***pronto soccorso*** casualty
**proprietario(a)** *m/f* owner
**proprio(a)** own
**prossimo(a)** next
**provare** to try; to test (*try out*); to try on (*clothes*)
**provvisorio(a)** temporary
**pubblicità** *f* advertisement
**pulito(a)** clean
**pulizia** *f* cleaning
**punto d'incontro** *m* meeting place

## Q

**qua** here
**qual(e)** what; which; which one
**qualche** some

# Italian – English

**qualcosa** something; anything
**qualcuno** someone; somebody
**qualità** *f* quality
**quando?** when?
**quanto(a)?** how much?
**quanti(e)?** how many?
**quartiere** *m* district
**quarto** *m* quarter
**quattro** four
**quei/quelli(e)** those; those ones
**quel(la)/quello(a)** that; that one
**questi(e)** these; these ones
**questo(a)** this; this one
**questura** *f* police station
**qui** here
**quindi** then; therefore
**quotidiano(a)** daily

## R

**rabbia** *f* anger; rabies
**raccomandare** to recommend
**radiografia** *f* x-ray
**raffreddore** *m* cold *(illness)*
**ragazza** *f* young woman; girlfriend
**ragazzo** *m* young man; boyfriend
**rallentare** to slow down
**rapido(a)** high-speed; quick
**recarsi alla cassa** pay at cash desk
**recentemente** recently
**reclamo** *m* complaint
**regalo** *m* present; gift
**Regno Unito** *m* United Kingdom
**regolare** regular; steady
**rendersi conto di** to realize
**reparto** *m* department; ward
**restare** to stay; to remain
**restituire** to return; to give back
**restituzione** *f* return; repayment
**resto** *m* remainder; change *(money)*
**ricaricare** to recharge *(battery)*
**ricetta** *f* prescription; recipe
**ricevere** to receive; to welcome
**ricevitore** *m* receiver *(phone)*
**ricevuta** *f* receipt
**richiedere** to require
**richiesta** *f* request
**riconoscere** to recognize

**ricordare** to remember
*non mi ricordo* I don't remember
**ricorrere a** to resort to
**ricoverare** to admit *(to hospital)*
**ridere** to laugh
**riduttore** *m* adaptor
**riduzione** *f* reduction
**riempire** to fill
**rifare** to do again; to repair
**rifiuti** *mpl* rubbish; waste
**rilasciato(a) a** issued at
**rimandare** to postpone
**rimanere** to stay; to remain
**rimborso** *m* refund
**rimettersi** to recover *(from illness)*
**ringraziare** to thank
**rinnovare** to renew
**rinunciare** to give up
**riparare** to repair
**riparazione** *f* repair
**ripetere** to repeat
**riposarsi** to rest
**risarcimento** *m* compensation
**riscaldare** to heat up *(food)*
**rischio** *m* risk
**riservare** to reserve
**riservato(a)** reserved
**riso** *m* rice; laugh
**risparmiare** to save *(money)*
**rispondere** to answer; to reply
**risposta** *f* answer
**ritardo** *m* delay
**ritirare** to withdraw
**ritornare** to return *(go back)*
**ritorno** *m* return
**riunione** *f* meeting
**rivolgersi a** to refer to *(for info)*
**rompere** to break
**rosa** pink
**rosa** *f* rose
**rossetto** *m* lipstick
**rosso(a)** red
**rotondo(a)** round
**rotto(a)** broken
**rovesciare** to spill; to knock over
**rubare** to steal
**rubinetto** *m* tap
**rumore** *m* noise
**rumoroso(a)** noisy
**ruota** *f* wheel

## S

**S** south *(abbr.)*
**sabato** *m* Saturday

# Italian – English

**sabbia** *f* sand
**sacchetto** *m* small bag
**sacco** *m* large bag
**sala** *f* hall; auditorium
**salario** *m* wage
**salato(a)** salted; savoury
**saldare** to settle *(bill)*; to weld
**saldi** *mpl* sale
**saldo** *m* payment; balance
**sale** *m* salt
**salire** to rise; to go up
***salire in*** to get in *(vehicle)*
**salone** *m* lounge; salon
**salotto** *m* living room; lounge
**saltare** to jump
**salute** *f* health
***salute!*** cheers!
**saluto** *m* greeting
**salvare** to rescue; to save *(life)*
**salve!** hello!
**salvietta** *f* serviette
**salvo** except; unless
**sapere** to know
**sapone** *m* soap
**sapore** *m* flavour; taste
**sbagliato(a)** wrong
**sbaglio** *m* mistake
**sbrigare** to hurry
**scadente** low *(standard, quality)*
**scadenza** *f* expiry
**scadere** to expire *(ticket, etc)*
**scaduto(a)** out-of-date; expired
**scala** *f* scale; ladder; staircase
**scaldare** to heat up
**scale** *fpl* stairs
**scarico(a)** flat *(battery)*
**scarpa** *f* shoe
**scatola** *f* box; tin
**scegliere** to choose
**scelta** *f* range; choice
**scendere** to go down
***scendere da*** to get off *(bus)*
**scheda** *f* slip *(of paper)*; card
***scheda telefonica*** phonecard
**sci** *m* ski; skiing
**sciare** to ski
**sciarpa** *f* scarf
**sciopero** *m* strike
**scomodo(a)** inconvenient; uncomfortable
**scomparire** to disappear
**scongelare** to defrost

**sconto** *m* discount
**scontrino** *m* ticket; receipt; chit
**scorso(a)** last
**scottatura** *f* burn
**Scozia** *f* Scotland
**scozzese** Scottish
**scrivere** to write; to spell
**scuola** *f* school
**scuro(a)** dark *(colour)*
**scusare** to excuse; to forgive
**scusarsi** to apologise
**scusi?** pardon?
**se** if; whether
**secondo(a)** second; according to
**sede** *f* head office
**sedersi** to sit down
**sedia** *f* chair
**seggiovia** *f* chair-lift
**segnale** *m* signal; road sign
**segnare** to score *(goal)*
**seguente** following
**seguire** to follow; to continue
**semaforo** *m* traffic lights
**semplice** plain; simple
**sempre** always; ever
**senso unico** one-way street
**senso vietato** no entry
**sentire** to hear
**sentirsi** to feel
**senza** without
**sera** *f* evening
**serio(a)** serious *(not funny)*
**servire** to serve
**servizio** *m* service; report *(in press)*
**servizi** *mpl* facilities; bathroom
**sesso** *m* sex
**sete** *f* thirst
***avere sete*** to be thirsty
**settembre** *m* September
**settimana** *f* week
**settimanale** weekly
**sì** yes
**sicurezza** *f* safety; security
**sicuro(a)** sure
**Sig.** Mr
**Sig.na** Miss
**Sig.ra** Mrs/Ms
**signore** ladies
**signori** gents
**silenzio** *m* silence
**simile (a)** similar to
**simpatico(a)** pleasant; nice
**singolo(a)** single
**sinistra** *f* left
**slacciare** to unfasten; to undo

**slegato(a)** loose (*not fastened*)
**smettere** to stop doing something
**soccorso** *m* assistance; help
**soldi** *mpl* money
**sole** *m* sun; sunshine
**solito: *di solito*** usually
**solo(a)** alone; only
**sono** I am (*to be*)
**sopra** on; above; over
**sorella** *f* sister
**sorpassare** to overtake
**sorridere** to smile
**sosta** *f* stop
**sotto** underneath; under; below
**sparire** to disappear
**speciale** special
**specialmente** especially
**spedire** to send; to dispatch
**spegnere** to turn off; to put out
**spendere** to spend (*money*)
**spento(a)** turned off; out (*light, etc*)
**sperare** to hope
**spese** *fpl* shopping; expenses
**spesso** often
**spettacolo** *m* show; performance
**spiaggia** *f* beach; shore
**spiccioli** *mpl* small coins; change
**spiegare** to explain
**spingere** to push
**sporco(a)** dirty
**sportello** *m* counter; door (*train, car*)
**sportivo(a)** informal (*clothes*)
**sposarsi** to get married
**sposato(a)** married
**squadra** *f* team
**stagione** *f* season
**stanco(a)** tired
**stanza** *f* room
**stare** to be; to keep
***stare attento(a) a...*** beware of...
***stare bene*** to be well
***come sta?*** how are you?
***stai zitto!*** keep quiet!
**stasera** tonight; this evening
**Stati Uniti** *mpl* United States
**stazione** *f* station; resort
**sterlina** *f* sterling; pound
**stesso(a)** same

**stitico(a)** constipated
**storico(a)** historic(al)
**strada** *f* road; street
**straniero(a)** foreign; foreigner
**strano(a)** strange
**su** on; onto; over; about; up
**sua** his; her(s); its; your(s) *(with f sing)*
**subito** immediately
**succedere** to happen
**succo** *m* juice
**sud** *m* south
**sue** his; her(s); its; your(s) *(with fpl)*
**suo(i)** his; her(s); its; your(s) *(with mpl)*
**suonare** to ring; to play
**suono** *m* sound
**superare** to exceed; to overtake
**supermercato** *m* supermarket
**supplemento** *m* supplement
**surgelato(a)** frozen
**sveglia** *f* alarm clock/call
**svegliare** to wake up
**svenire** to faint
**sviluppare** to develop *(photos)*

## T

**tabaccaio** *m* tobacconist's
**taglia** *f* size *(of clothes)*
**tagliare** to cut
**tangenziale** *f* ring road
**tanti(e)** so many
**tanto(a)** so much; so
**tardi** late
**tariffa** *f* tariff; rate
**tasca** *f* pocket
**tassa** *f* tax
**tasso** *m* rate
**tavola** *f* table; plank; board
**tazza** *f* cup
**tè** *m* tea
**telecomando** *m* remote control
**telefonare** to (tele)phone
**telefonata** *f* phone call
**telefonino** *m* mobile phone
**temperatura** *f* temperature
**tempo** *m* weather; time
**tenere** to keep; to hold
**termosifone** *m* heater
**terra** *f* earth; ground
**terzi** *mpl* third party
**terzo(a)** third
**tessera** *f* pass; season ticket; card
**testa** *f* head

# Italian – English

**tetto** *m* roof
**tirare** to pull
**toccare** to touch; to feel
***non toccare*** do not touch
**togliere** to remove; to take away
**tornare** to return; to come/go back
**torneo** *m* tournament
**torre** *f* tower
**tossire** to cough
**totale** *m* total *(amount)*
**tra** between; among(st); in
**tradurre** to translate
**traduzione** *f* translation
**tranquillante** *m* tranquillizer
**tranquillo(a)** quiet *(place)*
**trasferire** to transfer
**trasporto** *m* transport
**treno** *m* train
**trimestre** *m* term *(school)*
**triste** sad
**troppi(e)** too many
**troppo** too much; too
**trovare** to find
**tu** you *(familiar)*
**tuffarsi** to dive
**tutti(e)** all; everybody
**tutto(a)** everything; all

## U

**ubriaco(a)** drunk
**uccidere** to kill
**UE** *f* EU
**ufficio** *m* office; church service
**uguale** equal; even
**ultimo(a)** last
**un/uno(a)** a; an; one
**unione** *f* union
**uomo** *m* man
**uomini** gents
**usare** to use
**uscire** to go/come out
**uscita** *f* exit/gate
**utile** useful

## V

**va bene** all right *(agreed)*
**vacanza** *f* holiday(s)
**vagone** *m* carriage; wagon
**valido(a)** valid
**valido fino a...** valid until...
**valigia** *f* suitcase
**valore** *m* value; worth
***di valore*** valuable
**valuta** *f* currency
**vapore** *m* steam
**vecchio(a)** old
**vedere** to see
**vegetaliano(a)** vegan

**vegetariano(a)** vegetarian
**velenoso(a)** poisonous
**veloce** quick
**velocemente** quickly
**velocità** *f* speed
**vendere** to sell
**vendita** *f* sale
**venerdì** *m* Friday
**venire** to come
**verde** green
**verità** *f* truth
**vero(a)** true; real; genuine
**versamento** *m* payment; deposit
**versare** to pour
**vestirsi** to get dressed
**vestiti** *mpl* clothes
**vestito** *m* dress
**vetro** *m* glass (*substance*)
**via** *f* street; by (*via*)
**viaggiare** to travel
**viaggiatore** *m* traveller
**viaggio** *m* journey; trip; drive
**vicino(a)** near; close by
**videogioco** *m* computer game
**video-registratore** *m* video recorder
**vietato** forbidden
***vietato fumare*** no smoking
***vietato l'ingresso*** no entry
**vigili del fuoco** *mpl* fire brigade
**vigilia** *f* eve
**vincere** to win
**vino** *m* wine
**violentare** to rape
**visita** *f* visit
**visitare** to visit
**visto** *m* visa
**vita** *f* life; waist
**vivere** to live
**vivo(a)** live; alive
**volare** to fly
**voler dire** to mean
**volere** to want
**volo** *m* flight
**volta** *f* time
**vostro(a)** your; yours
**vuoto(a)** empty

## Z

**zanzara** *f* mosquito
**zia** *f* aunt
**zio** *m* uncle
**zona** *f* zone
***zona blu*** restricted parking zone
**zucchero** *m* sugar
**zuppa** *f* soup

Further titles in Collins' phrasebook range

Collins Gem Phrasebook

Also available as **Phrasebook CD Pack**

**Other titles in the series**

Arabic
Cantonese
Croatian
Czech
Dutch
French
German
Greek
Italian
Japanese
Korean
Latin American Spanish
Mandarin
Polish
Portuguese
Russian
Spanish
Thai
Turkish
Vietnamese

# Collins Easy: Photo Phrasebook

Also available as
**Phrasebook CD Pack**

**Other titles in the series**
Easy French
Easy Greek
Easy Italian

To order any of these titles, please telephone 0870 787 1732. For further information about all Collins books, visit our website: www.collins.co.uk